The

Maynooth Studies in Local History

SERIES EDITOR Raymond Gillespie

This volume is one of five short books published in the Maynooth Studies in Local History series in 2016. Like their predecessors they range widely, both chronologically and geographically, over the local experience in the Irish past. Chronologically they span the worlds of 16th-century Westmeath to those of Waterford in the early 20th century. Geographically, they range across the length of the country from Derry and Antrim to Waterford and Mallow in County Cork. Socially they move from the landed and elite ecclesiastical society of Sir John Keane and Thomas Ward, dean of Connor, to the social position of children who lost their mother in 19th-century Mallow and trade unionism in Derry in the 20th century. In doing so they reveal diverse and complicated societies of the local past, and the range of possibilities open to anyone interested in studying that past. Those possibilities involve the dissection of the local experience in the complex and contested social worlds of which it is part as people strove to preserve and enhance their positions within their local societies. Such studies of local worlds over such long periods are vital for the future since they not only stretch the historical imagination but provide a longer perspective on the evolution of society in Ireland and help us to understand more fully the complex evolution of the Irish experience. These works do not simply chronicle events relating to an area within administrative or geographically determined boundaries, but open the possibility of understanding how and why particular regions had their own personality in the past. Such an exercise is clearly one of the most exciting challenges for the future and demonstrates the vitality of the study of local history in Ireland.

Like their predecessors these five short books are reconstructions of the socially diverse worlds of the poor as well as the rich, women as well as men, children as well as adults and reconstruct the way in which those who inhabited those worlds lived their daily lives, often little affected by the large themes that dominate the writing of national history. In addressing these issues, studies such as those presented in these short books, together with their predecessors, are at the forefront of Irish historical research and represent some of the most innovative and exciting work being undertaken in Irish history today. Like the other volumes in this series, they provide models that others can follow, and convey the vibrancy and excitement of the world of Irish local history today.

Maynooth Studies in Local History: Number 124

The world of Thomas Ward: sex and scandal in late seventeenth-century Co. Antrim

Eamon Darcy

FOUR COURTS PRESS

Set in 10pt on 12pt Bembo by
Carrigboy Typesetting Services for
FOUR COURTS PRESS LTD
7 Malpas Street, Dublin 8, Ireland
www.fourcourtspress.ie
and in North America for
FOUR COURTS PRESS
c/o ISBS, 920 N.E. 58th Avenue, Suite 300, Portland, OR 97213

ISBN 978–1–84682–609–2

Printed in Ireland
by eprint, Dublin.

Contents

Acknowledgments

This study came about as a result of a two-year Irish Research Council Postdoctoral Fellowship entitled 'Oral and literate culture in early modern Ireland'. This led to the discovery of a curious manuscript, upon which this study is based, a record of proceedings by the Church of Ireland that led to the defrocking of a minister for adultery in the late 17th century. This source only recently came to be housed in the Representative Church Body Library and both Raymond Refaussé and Susan Hood were very welcoming and a great help throughout my time there. While researching my broader project on oral and literate culture I was based in the history department in Maynooth University where I had the good fortune to work with wonderful colleagues. I would like to thank them all for their collegiality, conviviality and enthusiasm. I am particularly grateful to Professor Raymond Gillespie for his advice and suggestions on both the project and this study. His thoughtful guidance has been a great help over the last few years and is truly appreciated.

Finally, I would like to thank my in-laws, my siblings, my parents, and my wife (who were all surprisingly supportive of my interest in 17th-century adultery), and my daughter (who is, thankfully, too young to know any better). As you know, I relished researching and writing this study and I hope you enjoy reading it.

Introduction: the world of Thomas Ward

We know very little about Thomas Ward. Biographical information compiled much later by Henry Cotton and John Leslie offers only a tentative glimpse of his life as a Church of Ireland minister. Ward graduated from Trinity College, Dublin, in 1662 and in the 1670s he served as prebendary of Mayne, Ballyclug and Maynooth until his final appointment as dean of Connor in 1679. In April 1694, his career in the Church of Ireland came to a rather ignominious end as he was deprived of his office for adultery.[1] We know, however, much more about the wider world in which Ward lived. His tenure as dean of Connor coincided with the Popish Plot of 1678–81, the Exclusion Crisis in 1679–81, and the war of 1689–91 and the many problems these crises posed to the Irish Protestant establishment.

By the end of the 17th century, the Church of Ireland in which Ward ministered had to contend with a number of issues. The fallout from the wars of the mid-17th century was, to a certain extent, still being felt before the succession of the Catholic James II in 1685 and the outbreak of the war of 1689–91. Williamite success gave way to a realization of the structural problems within the established Church of Ireland. Church buildings were in ruins, glebe lands had fallen idle and some of the clergy (and members of the laity) had either converted to Catholicism or left Ireland for England after James II's coronation. Throughout the 17th century, visitation reports noted the Church's poor revenues and these problems were further exacerbated by other difficulties such as the indifference of the laity, the improper appropriation of Church revenues, as well as absenteeism and pluralism among the clergy. As Anthony Dopping, the bishop of Meath, wrote in 1697: 'The state and condition of the Church of Ireland was never very good'. To make matters worse, Presbyterian communities were growing in strength and number, particularly in east Ulster where Ward was based. Scottish settlers readily settled on Irish Catholic lands that had been vacated after the withdrawal of the Jacobite army and practised Presbyterianism. A small number of newly appointed bishops within the Established Church aimed to tackle this problem. They were not only concerned with the plight of the institution but also the behaviour of the lower clergy and the wider laity, particularly in an era of alleged deliverance from popish tyranny.[2] A crucial issue remained in their minds, why did God punish Ireland's (and England's) Protestant communities with a Catholic monarch, James II, and why had he almost won the war against William?

This prompted much introspection and a concerted campaign, particularly in Dublin, to reform the laity's behaviour as their sins were blamed for incurring God's wrath. In the early 1690s, a number of prominent Church of Ireland clergymen, inspired by both the anniversary of the 1641 rebellion and contemporary unease about the leniency of the Treaty of Limerick, preached on the perils of Protestant misdeeds, sins and impiety, and called for greater moral discipline in light of the 'atheistical discourse and scurilous treatment of Holy things' in Ireland. A desire for the greater observance of the Sabbath led to the establishment of a number of societies for the reformation of manners in Dublin (others emerged in Drogheda, Kilkenny and Maynooth) that had links with like-minded groups in London. Thus, Ireland was 'swept up in the zest for reforming societies'. These movements offered a brief glimpse of Protestant unity in Ireland at a time of great tensions between Church of Ireland Protestants and Presbyterians. They punished Sabbath breakers and those who were caught cursing, profaning and swearing. This initiative was supported by the passage of two acts in 1695 that ensured the stricter observance of the Sabbath and penalized profane cursing and swearing. These societies hoped to raise awareness of the collective nature of sin and that communities also shouldered responsibility in the regulation and moderation of individuals' behaviour. These movements illustrated what could be achieved when the laity and clergy worked together, particularly in the heart of Protestant Ireland, Dublin.[3]

Ward's particular jurisdiction was more problematic. In contrast to what was happening in Dublin, where a number of bishops eager to reform the Church of Ireland continually visited and collaborated with one another, in east Ulster matters were not helped by the fact that Ward's superior, Bishop Thomas Hackett, was guilty of absenteeism. According to Walter Alison Phillips: 'The truth is that the annals of the Church of Ireland during the last four decades of the 17th century can show no bishop who more disgraced his office.' In his absence, Lemuel Matthews, the archdeacon of Down, administered the diocese but a number of undesirable people (in the eyes of the Church hierarchy), most notably Mrs Mary Cole and Mrs Catherine Hackett, the disgraced bishop's wife, were thought to play a prominent role locally. Throughout the 1680s, Hackett neglected his episcopal duties, preferring instead to stay in London. In order to facilitate his lifestyle, Hackett regularly sold livings to the highest bidder and under James II he appointed Catholic priests to church livings in return for an extension on his licence of absence from the diocese. His tenure as bishop exacerbated the deep-seated structural problems the Church of Ireland faced at the end of the 17th century in the diocese of Down and Connor. The Established Church at this time was in a strange position. The steady implementation of the penal laws in the 1690s and 1700s offered hope that its congregation would grow much larger but the lack of suitably trained (and behaved) clergymen and poor resources placed limits on what could be achieved. Thus, the diocese of Down and Connor was a serious concern to reformers because the region lacked episcopal leadership, which had a detrimental effect on the practice of Church of Ireland Protestantism in the eyes of some contemporaries.[4]

It is important to note that the Church was only one component, albeit an important one, of Ward's world. The local community stood at the heart of the early modern world and Ward, as minister, had a pivotal part to play. His parishioners attended his services (or at the very least they were supposed to attend his services), but they also supplied Ward with company, drink, food, friendship, news, and, no doubt, some of his neighbours irritated and annoyed Ward during his time as dean. Ward's role as a minister in the Established Church and his office of dean connected the locality to wider national political issues caused by the upheavals of the war of 1689–91 and international political tensions. There is an unrivalled opportunity to understand all these contexts to Ward's world by using the proceedings against him by the royal commission of 1694, which stripped him of his office for the infraction of adultery, as a keyhole through which we can view life and society in late 17th-century east Ulster. An abstract of the pleadings and proofs of the trial of Thomas Ward have survived and are now held by the Representative Church Body Library. The abstract contains 98 pages that describe the proceedings against Ward for his various misdemeanours. A closer inspection of the proceedings against Ward and the investigations of the commissioners, Anthony Dopping and William King, the bishops of Meath and Derry respectively, offers a valuable perspective on wider political, religious and social developments and daily life.[5] The purpose of this short book, therefore, is to delve a little deeper into the proceedings against Ward in order to gain an enriched view of late 17th-century Ireland.

The first chapter looks at the diocese of Down and Connor and outlines the structural problems the Established Church faced in the region and the steps taken by the clerical hierarchy to remedy these issues prior to defrocking Ward. The second chapter investigates the community that Ward represented, and was very much a part of, and how they reacted to the proceedings against him. Ward's behaviour as a minister had already been analysed, criticized, discussed and dissected by his parishioners and this evidence was a crucial part of the proceedings. Ward's reputation and his behaviour were both under suspicion. Thus, the final chapter looks at how contemporaries attempted to prove guilt in cases of adultery, fornication and infractions of a sexual nature. The proceedings against Ward offer an invaluable insight into communal and social relations; the interconnectedness of fame, reputation and the social order; and, finally, sexual politics in late 17th-century east Ulster.

1. The local and religious world of Thomas Ward

In the late 17th century, it was believed that the diocese of Down and Connor had long-standing links with the history of Christianity in Ireland. For example, in 1691, the prolific historian Laurence Echard hailed Downpatrick as 'one of the most ancient towns in Ireland' and the town was famed as the site of St Patrick's burial.[1] An increasingly diverse population regularly visited sacred sites connected to St Patrick on key days in the Christian calendar. The proximity of east Ulster to Scotland attracted settlers from highland and lowland Scotland and England. Their presence on the Chichester and Massereene estates alongside existing Irish communities meant that the region became one of the most cosmopolitan areas in the 17th century. It comprised Irish, English, Scottish, Catholic, Church of Ireland Protestant and Presbyterian communities. The purpose of this chapter is to look at the demographic changes that occurred in east Ulster during the second half of the 17th century and to investigate the response of the Church of Ireland to the resultant stresses these changes and wider political upheavals caused to the region.

East Ulster proved an attractive place for Scottish migrants due to its close proximity to Scotland. In the mid-1650s it was estimated that the average passage between Islandmagee in Co. Antrim and Scotland was only four hours.[2] Descriptions of the area in the latter half of the 17th century largely confirm the notion that a diverse community of Irish and Scottish people lived in east Ulster. In the 1650s, when the entire island of Ireland was mapped as part of the Down Survey project, Cromwellian cartographers captured the demographic range of the local population, which showed that some areas were quite mixed. For example, the barony of Cary in Co. Antrim consisted of both Irish and Scottish people and in Kilconway there was little to distinguish between the two communities as 'the inhabitants thereof are chiefly Scotts Protestants and Irish Papists who lived altogether in creaghts'.[3] In Kinalearty, Co. Down, the inhabitants were 'for the most part old Irish, many Scotts but few English'.[4] Other regions were less diverse. In Glenarm, Co. Antrim, the 'chiefest inhabitants' were all Scottish while in Lower Iveagh, Co. Down, 'the chiefest inhabitants whereof are Scots who by reason of the nearness of their country to these parts are growne very populous in this Barony'.[5] In the second half of the 17th century, 50,000 Scottish and 50,000 English settlers migrated to Ulster, while the 1690s and early 1700s witnessed a further 50,000 people flock to the region to fill vacated lands. By 1709 the population of Ulster probably stood at 480,000.[6] Thus, over the course of the late 17th and early 18th centuries the region witnessed a considerable influx of Scottish settlers who were largely Presbyterian and their presence unsettled and continually worried the Church of Ireland authorities. Despite this, relations between the three ethnic and religious communities were largely positive although tensions could erupt at times of politico-religious crisis or after failed harvests.[7]

Contemporaries keenly noted these demographic shifts in the late 17th century. In the 1680s, as part of a failed attempt to compile a detailed atlas, Moses Pitt, an English printer and bookseller, asked William Molyneux for information on Ireland. Although the venture collapsed due to rising costs, some of Molyneux's notes have survived.[8] Molyneux received a description of Co. Antrim from Richard Dobbs, a landlord from Kilroot parish. The Dobbs family had been there for four generations and a Mr Dobbs was listed as the owner of Castle Dobbs in Kilroot in the Books of Survey and Distribution for both 1641 and 1670. Their house, which had been much improved by Richard Dobbs (according to his own account), was situated close to Kilroot house, a residence of the bishop of Down and Connor. Dobbs considered himself an English man and he claimed that his family and about six others were the only English in the parish of Kilroot. The rest were 'all Presbyterians and Scotch, not one natural Irish in the parish'. The adjoining parish of Broad Island or Templecorran had a similarly strong Scottish and Presbyterian community living there, with the exception of the Church of Ireland parson and the clerk of the local church who were possibly father and son.[9] Dobbs explained that there were so few Irish living in Islandmagee because they 'were murdered by the Scottish inhabitants' during the 1640s.[10] In nearby Larne, the inhabitants were mostly Scottish and Presbyterian, although a small number of people attended the Church of Ireland there. The town of Glenarm by the 1680s was, according to Dobbs, slightly more diverse. The inhabitants were largely Scottish and Presbyterian while in the surrounding glens the population was mostly Irish and Catholic. These Irish, Dobbs argued, were 'more civilized' than the rest due to the influence of the local earl of Antrim.[11] While Dobbs' estimation of the number of Scottish people living in the region suggested a strong Presbyterian community there, it is necessary to point out that contemporary fears among Church of Ireland Protestants of dissenting sects in Ulster may have led to inflated estimates of their number.[12]

By the 1680s the diocese of Down and Connor still faced significant problems that arose from the wars of the mid-17th century. A survey of the parish structures made in 1657 as part of a scheme to reorganize parishes suggests that the ecclesiastical and financial structures of the Church were weak. The survey detailed how ministers were poorly paid and the churches severely neglected.[13] Crucially, the legacy of the wars of the 1640s was still apparent. Revenues had declined considerably, particularly in Co. Down. Between 1640 and 1657, Church livings in some parishes had collapsed. For example, the parish of Ballyphilip was worth £30 per annum in 1640 but by 1657 was of no value.[14] Tyrella parish's returns dropped from £40 in 1640 to £10 in 1657.[15] Not all of Down's parishes experienced such a sharp decrease in their livings and some reported only moderate losses, but the events of the 1650s took their toll on Church finances. In 1693, the archdeacon of Down, Lemuel Matthews, complained that the Established Church did not control enough of the tithes directly, a problem that had been exacerbated in the 1650s when Cromwellian soldiers were rewarded for their service out of Church coffers.[16] These soldiers were not alone and other members of the laity claimed some of the Church's revenues, which they then administered accordingly. Thus, some parishes had a salaried minister whose payments were organized by a member of the laity such as Arthur Moneypenny in Inch parish who funded the local minister's salary.[17] In other parishes, James Hamilton – later the earl of Clanbrassil – enjoyed the tithes but paid a stipend to the local minister.[18] In Comber parish Major Robert Ward enjoyed two-thirds of the tithes while the preacher received the other third.[19] In a small number of places ministers had access to glebe lands and farms upon which they could make a living. The overall picture painted by the 1657 report on the potential livings of Protestant clergymen in Co. Down, however, was grim.[20] Furthermore, many parishes had no resident minister or had no church building suitable for worship. In some cases the church consisted only of ruined walls.[21]

The 1657 survey of Co. Antrim painted a similar picture although the Church livings suffered a more modest decline from the wars of the mid-17th century. Perhaps the worst affected was the parish of Billy whose income dropped from £150 per annum to £100. Jeremy O'Quin served as minister there having been appointed by the Cromwellians specifically because he could preach in Irish.[22] The same problems that affected Co. Down clergy also existed in Antrim. The majority of the parishes had no glebe. This made it difficult for ministers to make a living. Only a small handful of parishes, such as Armoy, Ballyrashane, Glenarm and Milltown had enough glebe lands for the minister to farm.[23] Similarly, many of the church buildings in Antrim were either ruined or in a decrepit state. The administration of the tithes and the payment of ministers was also controlled largely by the Cromwellian regime and important local lords such as the Conway and Chichester families. In sum, there were not enough ministers and an inadequate number of safe church buildings in the diocese of Down and Connor by the end of the 1650s. To make matters worse, there were only two schools actively used in the diocese (in the towns of Antrim and Downpatrick). Although four Protestant schoolmasters lived in Co. Antrim there was no school building in which they could work.[24] In the words of the commissioners who compiled these reports, in 'most of the said parishes … their condition is not suitable either for sufficiency of maintenance to the ministers or conveniency for resort of the parishioners unto'.[25]

In 1660, after the Restoration of the Stuart monarchy, the diocese of Down and Connor was a specific concern among the Church hierarchy because of the growth of dissenting sects in the region. In order to address the situation, Jeremy Taylor was appointed as bishop. Many contemporaries held Taylor's devotional writings in the highest regard with his *Rule and exercises of holy living* (London, 1650) appearing in 14 editions between 1650 and 1700.[26] Taylor's remit was to enforce the organization and doctrine of the Established Church in east Ulster in the face of growing strength of the Presbyterian community, or as John Bramhall, the archbishop of Armagh, succinctly put it, for the 'reformation of that schismatical part of the country'. In 1660, there were between 30 and 40 Presbyterian ministers claiming rights as incumbents in the diocese. Aware of their hostility to episcopacy, Taylor held a diocesan synod, but only two Presbyterian preachers attended. This allowed Taylor to declare the other cures vacant and ready to be filled by episcopally ordained clergy.[27] To promote doctrinal orthodoxy and accommodate the religious needs of the laity, Taylor worked closely with the Conway family, the south Antrim landlords and Taylor's patrons, but he still had to contend with stubborn beliefs among the laity that did not fully reflect Church teachings.[28] Taylor took a keen interest in some of the more dramatic supernatural encounters of the laity and he investigated at least two ghostly apparitions in the diocese in the years 1662 and 1663. The first reported apparition was witnessed by Francis Taverner, a tenant of Arthur Chichester; he claimed to have seen the ghost of James Haddock. Haddock's ghost re-appeared before Taverner several times and eventually Taverner sought the assistance of James South (Chichester's chaplain) and Lewis Down (minister of Belfast) who brought the matter before the bishop. The following year David Hunter, one of Taylor's herdsmen, claimed to have seen a ghost of a woman whose first husband died during the wars of the 1640s. She subsequently married a soldier who failed to provide sufficiently for her son from her first marriage or any of her subsequent children with the soldier. She urged Hunter to go to her first-born son and tell him to dig under a hearth whereupon he would find 28s. This would allow him to pay for her funeral charges and give his family greater financial comfort. Having heard that her wishes were fulfilled (despite some reluctance on Hunter's part) the vision disappeared and Hunter heard the 'most delicate Musick as she went off'. The investigators could not determine whether these two apparitions were real or whether they were a product of 'drunkenness' or 'melancholy'. Such ghostly apparitions were problematic for clergymen as the power of interpretation lay firmly in the hands of the laity to understand the meaning of the supernatural appearances. These ghostly stories and Taylor's investigation of their authenticity reveal the tensions between doctrinally educated clergymen and the laity whose beliefs did not always conform to institutional orthodoxy.[29]

Bishop Taylor's investigations reflected the inherent tensions between popular and orthodox religious practices but they also illustrated the reliance by the laity on the supernatural to explain the early modern world. Commentators on the region noted the religious practices of the lower social orders at a time of great upheaval within the Church of Ireland. For example, the Presbyterian minister, Patrick Adair, scrutinized the religious experiences at a popular level in east Ulster in his history of the Presbyterian Church in Ireland. Adair's narrative hinted that there was considerable demand for skilled preachers in the region. His account, albeit to be taken with a pinch of salt, indicates that the 'common sort of people' keenly approved of and demanded religious instruction.[30] Similarly, in 1682, Dobbs hinted at strong folk beliefs in the sanctity of local religious shrines and their popularity among all denominations in the area. There was a considerable devotion to St Patrick and Dobbs recorded that near Downpatrick there was a small hut built from limestone 'wherein tradition says St Patrick lodged … old people say they had seen a stone there (a hard pillow) wherein appeared a hollow, where the saint used to lay his head'. A nearby well, St Patrick's well, was particularly popular on Midsummer Eve where yearly more than 300 people came to wash and pray and then proceed on their 'bare knees' to climb a rock called St Patrick's chair. Similarly, in Larne another well drew Irish and Scottish inhabitants together every Midsummer's Eve.[31]

Despite this popular devotion many of the problems that blighted the Church of Ireland in 1657 still remained in 1682 according to Richard Dobbs. For example, in Templecorran there was a 'handsome church' but no churchmen, while the local Presbyterian community flourished. In Larne, despite the presence of a local dean, the Presbyterian community was particularly strong. Every Sunday sermon was heard twice and once during the week, 'and generally the people will not omit Christening with their own minister, supposing the children to be born into the Solemn League and Covenant'.[32] Thus, even before the turbulence of the Williamite succession in Ireland the presence of Scottish communities was seen as a considerable threat. Accordingly the Church hierarchy was concerned about the religious beliefs of local communities and the weak state of the Established Church.

A visitation conducted in February 1694 revealed how the perennial problems that faced the diocese from a structural perspective had still not been dealt with. Many of the key settlements in the diocese lacked a suitable church building such as Donegore and Islandmagee in Co. Antrim. Similarly, ministers were frequently absent. The visitation noted how there was no resident dean in Carrickfergus (a position Thomas Ward should have filled) nor was there an incumbent in Ballymoney. In some places where a resident minister could be found the report cast aspersions on their ability to serve the parishioners. The curate in Ballymoney was practically blind and incapable of fulfilling his duties. To make matters worse, ministers were not deployed in areas where they could exert a useful influence on behalf of the Church. For example, an (unidentifiable) Irish-speaking minister was employed as curate in Ardclinis but the commissioners believed that he would have been better suited to the parish on Rathlin Island 'where a great many Irish Protestants live and are apostatized in want of service'.[33] The archdeacon of Down, Lemuel Matthews blamed the structural weakness of the Church for the lack of success in maintaining Church of Ireland Protestant congregations in the diocese. As ministers lacked glebes and manse houses this excused 'many of ye Clergy of ye said diocese from residence on their respective livings, whereby divine service, hospitality & relief of ye poor have been neglected, & are occasion of ye general non-conformity'. Furthermore, in many regions the Presbyterian church had grown so strong, local inhabitants had become dissenters and would not serve as church wardens, thus 'the Churches goe out of repair & the decayd ones are not repayred'.[34]

The diocese of Down and Connor was perhaps one of the more cosmopolitan dioceses in Ireland, consisting of an ethnically and religiously diverse population that lived in both integrated and segregated communities. Thus, the diocese became a battleground between rival Protestant communities in an era of Presbyterian growth and heated conversations about Presbyterian tolerance, a proposal that was roundly rejected by several Church of Ireland bishops in an attempt to maintain and cultivate their political and religious supremacy. The financial and structural problems that weakened the Church of Ireland in the late 17th century were of considerable concern to both clerical and lay elites. The vulnerability of the Church is reflected in the careers of its individual bishops. After Taylor's efforts to reform religious practices and tackle the long-seated problems in the Church, his successors did not follow suit. Despite this, the popular religious practices of the lower social orders did not wane but adapted to the profound demographic and political changes that affected the region. This led many within the Established Church to believe that both Catholicism and Presbyterianism prospered as a result of the weakness of the Church of Ireland.

★ ★ ★

The challenges the Church of Ireland faced in the diocese were not helped by the absenteeism of the bishop, Thomas Hackett, throughout the 1680s. Hackett had risen to prominence during the restoration of the Stuart monarchy and preached a sermon before a convocation of the Church of Ireland in May 1661 when he had been appointed as dean of Cork on the recommendation of James Butler, the duke of Ormond. He resigned from this position a year later and returned to London to become rector of St Christopher's, vicar of Cheshunt in Hertfordshire and then the chaplain-in-ordinary of Charles II. In 1672 he became the bishop of Down and Connor and the beginning of his administration was largely unexceptional. He befriended the local nobility, most notably Lord Conway, but he disliked Ireland and in 1680 he travelled to Bath, claiming ill health prevented his return. It became clear by 1686 that Hackett's neglect of his diocese had been detrimental to the Church of Ireland. The newly appointed lord lieutenant, Henry Hyde, the earl of Clarendon, was not keen to extend Hackett's licence of absence but Hackett refused to return to Ireland.[35]

His absenteeism earned him the sobriquet of 'bishop of Hammersmith' – a testament to his time spent in London away from his diocese.[36]

Concerned about events in Down and Connor, Queen Mary set up a royal commission in December 1693 to prosecute those deemed responsible for the neglect of the diocese in light of the 'severall complaints [that] are made daily of many grievous offences abuses and enormitys to have been committed by Dr Thomas Hackett'.[37] Three bishops who had gained a reputation for reform and rebuilding the Church of Ireland were appointed to this commission (although only two served).[38] The first, Anthony Dopping, bishop of Meath, rose to prominence in the midst of the Williamite wars. He promoted the interests of the Established Church in the Jacobite parliament of 1689 and opposed the repeal of the acts of settlement and explanation that would have restored Catholic landowners to lands confiscated in the mid-17th century. In the aftermath of the Williamite wars, Dopping along with William King, Narcissus Marsh, Samuel Foley and Nathaniel Foy formed a group of reform-minded bishops who wished to rebuild the Church of Ireland.[39] William King joined Dopping on the royal commission. Since his appointment as bishop of Derry, King had worked tirelessly to improve the Established Church in his diocese even going so far as to procure disued Irish-language bibles and common prayer books for his flock. He was surprised at the inaction of his subordinates and wrote to Foley exclaiming, 'I admonished the clergy as to residence, providing curates, preaching constantly & catechizing according to the canon conferring with recusants &c which some did not relish'.[40] King felt frustrated by the inactivity of his fellow clergymen in Down and Connor, confessing to Foley that 'it is a great grief to me that I am obliged to drive & whip people to their duty'.[41]

The commissioners quickly blamed Hackett's absenteeism for the rise of the Presbyterian movement in the region as they worked to rebuild the Church in the diocese. Hackett was indicted in six articles before the commissioners and the investigation into his episcopacy revealed how poorly administered the Church of Ireland was during the 1680s. The first issue that arose was his non-residency. Hackett defended himself by claiming that he was 'under great infirmity of body and therefore advised to repair into England'.[42] It later transpired that Hackett had appointed a Catholic priest to a Church living in the diocese in the late 1680s in order to obtain a renewal of his licence of absence from the Catholic lord deputy, Tirconnell.[43] The effect of his absence was detrimental according to the seven witnesses who testified against Hackett. They argued that Hackett had not performed his episcopal duties of confirmation and ordination. Joseph Wilkins, for example, claimed that 'tho there was great neede of confirmation this deponent being forced to admit several persons to receive the sacrament without being confirmed they being extremely desireous to be admitted to the receiveing thereof, and could not be confirmed for want of an opportunity'.[44] Another deponent claimed that both he and another man wished to be ordained by the bishop and waited for the bishop's appearance for seven years, 'which

was a great discouragement'.[45] Hackett, aware that the commissioners were
about to investigate him for non-residency, quickly returned to Ireland and set
out to restore his reputation in the diocese and perform key episcopal duties
that he had neglected during his absence. He hastily convened a service in
Lisburn church and quickly confirmed a small number of people in order to
'take some of the scandal and reproach that such his neglects had brought on
him'.[46] Despite his efforts some parents refused to allow their children to be
confirmed as they believed that Hackett was incapable of performing the office
'with due seriousness and decency'.[47] Thus, the commissioners argued, Hackett's
actions further weakened the position of the Church in Down and Connor
because many who were willing to be confirmed had to travel to the diocese of
Dromore. There they found out that the bishop of Dromore refused to do so
because they did not have a letter from Hackett sanctioning their confirmation
in another diocese.

It quickly became apparent that Hackett's efforts to cover the tracks of his
absenteeism were in vain. As part of his desperate attempts to compensate for his
absence he called upon those who wished to be ordained as ministers to attend
an ordination service at Lisburn church. The ceremony was a shambles. Hackett
had a limited grasp of what he was supposed to do and had to be instructed by
his archdeacon, Lemuel Matthews, and by John Hart who was asked to hold the
Book of Common Prayer open so that the bishop could read from it. Hart, it
was alleged, pointed out the relevant sections for the bishop to read aloud but
frequently misled Hackett in this regard.[48] At one point in the ordination service
Hackett mistakenly offered the candidates the Bible to read when he was supposed
to place his hands on their head and utter a blessing instead. Matthews quickly
corrected Hackett but the elderly and frail bishop was unable to hold his hands
on the candidates' heads as he blessed them. Matthews' frequent admonition 'my
lord you must keep your hands on' and Hackett's inability to utter the blessing in
full (he omitted the key line: 'and whose sins thou dost retain they are retained')
meant that the proceedings were seen to lack the level of solemnity the audience
expected.[49] One of the witnesses at the ceremony claimed that the bishop
appeared as a 'man that … understood [not] what he was doing' and that he was
easily influenced by the archdeacon of Down, Lemuel Matthews.[50] From the
commissioners' investigation it appeared that not only was Hackett responsible
for the severe decline in the numbers of people being ordained and confirmed in
the diocese, it also appeared that Hackett was unfit to exercise his office. He had
been heavily influenced, they argued, by his wife, Catherine, and by Mrs Mary
Cole in the governance of his diocese and he had allowed Matthews to usurp his
authority. The commissioners duly expelled Hackett from his diocese and later
excommunicated his wife for neglect of the diocese.[51]

Despite Hackett's absence, the Church did not collapse, as others stepped in
to administer the diocese. While their intentions may have been honourable, the
commissioners believed that some had acted improperly. The commissioners

had been charged by Queen Mary to investigate the causes of the abuses in the diocese fully and to prosecute any members of the clergy whom they found complicit in its neglect. Thus, they turned their attentions to Matthews.

★ ★ ★

Lemuel Matthews had worked in the diocese of Down and Connor for a considerable number of years by the time of the investigation by the royal commission. In 1661, he was appointed as the schoolmaster of Carrickfergus and later became chaplain to Jeremy Taylor while he was bishop of Down and Connor. From 1666 Matthews held numerous benefices in the diocese. He was vicar of Aghagallon, Aghalee, Glenavy, and prebendary of Carncastle and in 1674 he was appointed as archdeacon of Down.[52] Before Anthony Dopping and William King, Matthews stood accused of neglecting his responsibilities and of usurping the authority of the absentee bishop.

The first charge claimed that Matthews had neglected 'several distinct rectories or parishes' across the diocese and that he had not resided in any of his cures for 18 or 19 years.[53] Fifteen witnesses testified on this matter and the overwhelming majority agreed with the charge, including a number of his fellow clergymen.[54] For example, David Maxwell claimed that Matthews never resided in any of his cures after his appointment as the archdeacon of Down and instead 'lived for the most part either in Lisburn or Dublin'.[55] Matthews defended his record by claiming that many of the problems the commissioners encountered already existed upon his appointment in the 1660s and that he had been unable to reclaim any of the lost properties and churches from Catholic and Presbyterian residents in the diocese as a result of the troubles of the 1640s and the 1650s. Lisburn, he argued, offered an ideal location for him to 'attend ministerial offices' in his parishes and he would later claim that he did not need to reside in parochial livings as he served as chancellor of Down.[56] The second charge claimed that Matthews deliberately left vicars without endowments and left several cures vacant. This caused the 'neglect of performing all ministerial offices therein' and had a direct effect on the local population who now 'have forsaken the communion of the Church of Ireland'.[57] Twelve witnesses provided evidence on this point and they all believed that Matthews' neglect had catastrophic consequences. John Fitzsimons from Kilclief parish alleged that a number of local families had converted to Catholicism and to Presbyterianism for want of religious instruction and a 'resident minister'. Fitzsimons testified that he asked a fellow parishioner why he had brought his children to Mass, Leek replied: 'He would serve God one way or another.'[58] Another deponent from Drumbeg parish claimed that the lack of a resident curate there meant that many parishioners have 'gone to Presbyterian meetings and others to Mass'. Worship in this parish seemed particularly haphazard as it was claimed that many attended church on Sundays 'in expectation of Divine Service' but no minister would appear.[59] While Matthews accepted the fact that no vicarages were endowed in his archdeaconry, he claimed that this was not his responsibility and he repeated his earlier point that the majority of the parishes he governed were 'long before [his] time, Recusants or obstinate dissenters' and that he had attempted to encourage them to attend local services.[60]

Matthews' defence hinged on the fact that it was not his sole responsibility to regenerate the Church of Ireland in east Ulster and that he needed cooperation from the laity. He accused his parishioners and the local authorities of failing to fulfil their duties and obligations to the Church. The 'country' inhabitants, he argued, refused to return to their churches in the afternoons for religious instruction as they had to travel too far from their 'distant dwellings'. Furthermore, when he heard that William Ambrose, a local Presbyterian minister, had preached at Hillsborough, Matthews claimed that he enlisted two justices of the peace to arrest Ambrose only to be warned that he had to 'forbear prosecution against the said Ambrose or other Presbyterian preachers'.[61] While Matthews was eager to blame local lay authorities for the failure to prosecute dissenters, John Fitzsimons told the commission that some were reluctant to enter into a lawsuit with Matthews because of his belligerent and hostile personality.[62] Matthews did not answer the charge that many churches under his auspices did not provide services on Christmas day yet some of the local parishioners spoke of their disappointment at the lack of worship on key dates in the Church calendar. Crucially, John McNeal claimed, 'he does not know that ever the said Lemuel Matthews catechised any of his parishioners in his life'. The lack of religious instruction had led to the growth of Presbyterianism in Hillsborough parish, according to McNeal. Now there was a Presbyterian minister 'where there was none before'.[63] Thus, the commission accused Matthews of neglecting his pastoral duties. They claimed that for 'many years' he had not taken care to visit the sick, to christen children, or to bury the dead. Some of the slack, the commission claimed, was taken up by neighbouring ministers but they could not get to everyone thus: 'Several of the children of the said parishes might have died unbaptized and many of the dead might be buried without the office of the dead'. They provided one clear example of Matthews' pastoral neglect: 'You were desired to visit a person that was sick, and pray with her [and] her family, where there were 12 Protestants but you delayed and refused to do it.'[64] Matthews anticipated that these claims referred specifically to his alleged neglect of Kilclief parish and explained his conduct by the fact that his curate had to attend personal business in Dublin and that he had appointed a replacement to tend to the sick, christenings and burials and he expressed surprise that there was a problem in Kilclief as nobody had complained to him about this matter.[65] It appeared that Matthews had drastically underestimated the extent of discontent in Kilclief parish toward him. John Fitzsimons again testified to Matthews' neglect of his duties and it became clear that the dying woman referred to in the commission's charge was Fitzsimons' mother. Fitzsimons duly informed others within the parish of Matthews' poor treatment of his mother; John McNeal, for example, testified that he had heard of Matthews' behaviour from Fitzsimons.[66] The commissioners were equally concerned with the reputation of the institutional Church, thus Fitzsimons' public complaints about Matthews' behaviour caused some anxiety.

Apart from neglect there were also allegations of corruption against Matthews. It quickly emerged that those who served under Matthews were underpaid and underappreciated. John McNeal informed the commissioners that many of the curates hired by Matthews were not 'fitly qualified' and that those who were able to serve were poorly paid, 'nor were they well paid what was promised them'. Matthews had earlier been accused of simony and of promoting his nephew, Philip Matthews, but the commissioners also raised other concerns. It was alleged that Matthews had usurped the authority of the bishop by issuing blank marriage licences under the episcopal seal to be sold throughout the country without oaths or bonds being taken or without their correct recording in the local registry. Matthews, once again, blamed somebody else for this problem and claimed that he had appointed a 'worthy clergyman' to administer and record marriage licences as it had 'been always practised and allowed' in Down and Connor. This allowed the unnamed 'worthy clergyman' to visit betrothed couples and administer oaths and grant licences more easily. Matthews' nephew corroborated his uncle's account but three other witnesses contradicted this version of events. Perhaps the most damning testimony came from Francis Wotton who took care of the diocesan registers and stated that the licences were not properly administered.[67] The ability to easily grant marriage licences could, potentially, facilitate intermarriages that were expressly forbidden by both Church and secular authorities; however, in reality, the rule was rarely enforced.

In the end, the commissioners suspended Matthews from his prebend of Carncastle and the chancellorship of Down, and deprived him of the office of archdeacon of Down for his 'enormous' neglect of his cures and his non-residency. The commissioners were so exasperated by Matthews' behaviour they also excommunicated him for refusing to prove his title to the prebend of Carncastle. Matthews later hinted that their actions were personal and spoke of their 'unusual and rigorous dealings against me'.[68] He spent the rest of his life challenging the decision made by Dopping and King and the legality of their commission. Eventually, he was restored to his prebend (but not his archdeaconry) after a sustained campaign on his part that had wider ramifications in Anglo-Irish politics in light of the growing controversy over Poynings' Law and the rights of the Irish parliament.[69] Matthews complained that he had not incurred any penalty under ecclesiastical or civil law. He justified his non-residency by stating that as chancellor of the cathedral church he was excused from parochial residence. His excommunication meant that he had been deprived of his 'natural defence and the right of a Protestant in appealing from their said sentences', something that had been guaranteed by William III. This exposed him, he argued, as 'an aged priest and dignitary of the church to starving or beggery' and deprived him of the benefit of the law.[70] Matthews deliberately played on this issue because it exposed an anomaly between the Irish and English legal codes. On 16 December 1689, after the accession of William III, the king issued a declaratory act (*The act declaring the rights and liberties of the subject*) that outlawed the use of royal commissions in England to deprive and excommunicate ministers and bishops in the Church of England because they prevented the right of appeal.[71] Such commissions, it was claimed, could be used to remove suitable ministers and introduce 'popery and slavery' as had occurred in the reign of James II. Matthews argued that this statute was also in force in Ireland.[72] In the early 1700s the English house of commons was already on high alert because of William Molyneux's *The case of Ireland's being bound by acts of Parliament in England, stated* (Dublin, 1698). Molyneux argued that certain English statutes (such as the prohibition of high commissions ecclesiastical in English common law) did not extend to Ireland as they needed to be confirmed by the 'ancient right' of the Irish parliament.[73] Molyneux touched a nerve in England and Matthews hoped to exploit these concerns in order to exonerate himself. He argued that *The act declaring the rights and liberties of the subject* was declaratory of common law and thus was in force in Ireland under the terms of Poynings' Law, or, in the words of one of Matthews' supporters: 'The said *Irish* commission ecclesiastical … is of like nature with the *English* commission, and was and is illegal, and pernicious.'[74]

Matthews' attempts to be restored to his former benefices were undermined by the anonymous publication of *The proceedings against Archdeacon Lemuel Matthews at the Regal Visitation held at Lisburn* (n.p., 1703). Members of the Irish political hierarchy may have been involved in its publication as a record of the proceedings against Matthews is part of the private papers of Sir Cyril Wyche who served as one of the lords justice (alongside William Duncombe and Henry, Lord Capel) while the royal commission investigated events in the diocese of Down and Connor.[75] While there is no evidence to suggest that Wyche was directly responsible for the printing of the proceedings against Matthews the key point to note is that its appearance was detrimental to Matthews' cause. He quickly recognized that a smear campaign had begun against him (presumably orchestrated by King's supporters) and he promised a reward to any who would provide him with information about the author or printer of the 'false and malicious pamphlet'.[76] In a subsequent open letter to William King, published in 1703, Matthews complained that he had been denied access to copies of the commission under which he was tried and to copies of the testimonies of those who deposed against him. Matthews once again challenged the legality of the court and accused King of deliberately excommunicating him from the Church thereby preventing him from lodging a formal appeal.[77]

Matthews hoped that he could encourage King to delve into his conscience and rectify his past mistakes: 'Consider that you are a *man*; and as such you might have been *mistaken* in your grievous acts and decrees given against me; and that if by your *mistakes* you have wronged me, you ought as a *Christian to acknowledge your error*.'[78] The effect of his deprivation and suspension was expressed in revealing terms. Matthews claimed that he had been deprived of his 'good name, by your [King's] defamatory articles and libels … upon pretence for reformation of my manners'. Thus, he was left 'naked' and 'exposed' to his enemies. Not only had he been deprived of his living, his good name, but also his 'means of salvation … and also of the best comfort of a Christian in his life and at his death'.[79] Despite his protestations the commissioners believed that both Hackett and Matthews had contributed to the serious decline of the Church in east Ulster. In the words of Queen Mary, their actions had caused great 'scandal' to the Established Church as the commissioners worked to restore its reputation. After the proceedings against Matthews were finished, Dopping wrote to the Co. Antrim landlord, John Skeffington, the Presbyterian Viscount Massereene, to thank him for his help in assisting the royal commission in their prosecution of Hackett and Matthews. Presumably shocked by what he and King had discovered, Dopping refused to commit the details to paper, instead offering to give 'a more full accompt when I see you'. In the meantime, Dopping asked Massereene for a list of other 'bad clergy in the diocese'. Dopping was frustrated because the local community who 'keep us in the dark' regarded both him and King as 'strangers'.[80] This was the sort of collaboration and co-operation that could occur among the Protestant communities of east Ulster in an era of widespread concern over the laity's behaviour. Massereene had delicately negotiated his way as a Presbyterian onto the Privy Council and survived Ormond's suspicions in the 1680s. Thus, Massereene was eager to assist the Church of Ireland hierarchy in order to protect his own interests at a time of great tensions in east Ulster, or he may have been inspired by the burgeoning reform of manners movement in Dublin. Thus, Thomas Ward's world witnessed both conflict and collaboration between Church of Ireland Protestants and Presbyterians in an era of remarkable resilience of popular religious practices among the lower social orders. At the heart of Ward's world, however, were the local community and the institutional Church that suffered considerably at the hands of Hackett and Matthews and the 'scandal' they caused. To address this 'scandal' among the laity the commissioners' attention would soon turn to Ward.

2. Fame, reputation and talk in east Ulster

The commissioners were on high alert because of the extent of gossip about Hackett's and Matthews' behaviour that brought shame to the Church. They may have been 'strangers' to the diocese but they quickly heard numerous critical stories about Hackett's behaviour during the ordination of new ministers. It transpired that Hackett was also unaware that the candidates for ordination did not inspire confidence among the laity, one of whom, John Gayer, was known locally as a 'menial servant' to Lemuel Matthews.[1] To make matters worse, eyebrows were raised during communion when Hackett drank from the cup and exclaimed loudly either 'this is base wine' or 'this is the basest wine I ever drunk in my life'. Hackett's distaste for the communion wine clearly registered with the local curate as the next time he conducted service in Lisburn, he enjoyed the (presumably improved) communion wine a little too much. Allegedly when taking the sacrament he drank 'to a great excess' and called the service to a halt prematurely without administering the final blessing. These incidents 'gave great offence to many godly and well disposed persons who were then there and were of great scandal to himself and the Episcopal order'.[2] The final charge put before Hackett by the royal commission was that 'the general fame of … the several articles [accusing Hackett of neglect] aforesaid are true'. 'Fame' here worked in two ways. Hackett did not know what Gayer's reputation or 'fame' was and Hackett was accused both of committing the offences and of having the reputation for committing the offences. This latter issue brought scandal to both Hackett as a person and to the institution of the Established Church. The purpose of this chapter, therefore, is to look in greater detail at the issue of fame in the proceedings of the royal commission in 1694, which will provide a unique insight into an early modern community.

We know of fame from literary sources, particularly elegies to various nobles that proclaimed their deeds and their fame would be handed down to posterity. Public fame, or *fama*, however was not simply a literary construct but something that reflected social discourse at a local level. It could involve rumour and idle talk but it also reflected the local community's opinion of, and knowledge about, its individual members; understandably, one's public or common fame may not always have been positive. Within the spectrum of public fame intersected a number of other key concepts of the early modern world. It involved honour, social status and the social order, shame as well as oral culture and all its performative and informative components. Public fame was closely reported and therefore moderated an individual's behaviour; people had to act

appropriately, particularly before other members of the court of local opinion.
It is important, therefore, to consider that public fame does not simply entail
gossip, rather it comprised communal conversations that defined and facilitated
social relations and reflected one's place in the social hierarchy. This gossip or,
to use a less pejorative term, talk, was one of the most immediate aspects of
people's daily lives and a salient component in the construction of their mental
world. As one's public fame reflected one's social standing and therefore one's
credibility, public fame also intersected with legal definitions regarding eyewitness testimonies as deponents' statements could be utilized or disregarded
because of their public fame.[3]

Public fame or reputation was legally defined and served a key role in English
common law courts in Ireland. A person's reputation could provide a reason
for arrest after a crime was committed. In 1638, Sir Richard Bolton informed
justices of the peace that if a felony was committed, JPs could arrest 'every man
… that be of evil fame' although it was preferable if one had a concrete reason
to suspect that they were guilty of the crime. The common fame of a vagrant
or an idle person was that they were of an unworthy character thus, 'to live
idelely and vagrant is good cause of suspicion'.[4] In criminal proceedings, Bolton
argued that if part of a person's testimony was proven to be false, then 'he is not
much to be credited in the residue of his information'. Those guilty of perjury
or even accused of perjury are not to be trusted either 'for the old saying is once
forsworne ever forlorne'.[5] Such instances may have not always been recorded by
hand but reported by word of mouth. Therefore, public fame both recorded and
circulated vital local information about individuals' behaviour and character.
Justices of the peace had to be aware of this public fame before arresting or
questioning someone. In the same way, Hackett should have known that Gayer's
standing was not adequate to be a minister. Hackett should have behaved in a
manner that would have led to a positive public fame. His behaviour should
have reflected his status as a bishop because public fame and the social order
often went hand in hand. While Bolton sketched out tangible ways to measure
somebody's credibility the proceedings against Thomas Ward provide us with
further evidence about how reputation and credibility could be measured
practically from a legal perspective.

★ ★ ★

Thomas Ward first appeared before the commissioners at the proceedings against
Hackett. His evidence confirmed suspicions that Hackett had neglected his
duties in the diocese. Ward claimed that there were no episcopal acts performed
by Hackett from May 1680 until May 1692 and that the bishop had not visited
some of the towns in his diocese for 14 years.[6] Ward had served as dean of
Connor since 1679 and he was reasonably well connected within the Church
as his brother, Michael Ward, was appointed bishop of Ossory in 1678. Michael

Ward was 'greatly esteemed for learning and sound judgement' but his brother did not have the same reputation among his colleagues or the laity.[7]

Ward was brought before the commissioners and was charged with 22 offences that covered two key areas. The first concerned Ward's administrative duties. For example, the 19th article against Ward accused him of neglecting the church of Islandmagee and for allowing it to fall into decay despite the fact that £100 had been raised locally for its upkeep. Ward denied that he had been inactive in this matter. He believed that his efforts were undermined by the lack of cooperation from locals. He reminded the commissioners that the inhabitants of Islandmagee were 'popishly inclined' and uninterested in Church of Ireland Protestantism. The evidence provided on this point was inconclusive as only one witness was called by the commissioners and he could not testify as to whether the church in Islandmagee was 'ruinous or in repair'.[8] Like Hackett and Matthews, Ward was also accused of non-residency and it was alleged that he had not visited many of his parishes for at least a year. Ward claimed that he had been ordered to live in Lisburn by Hackett and Matthews since 1692 in order to assist the bishop with his duties and that he had made provisions for a curate to visit the parishes he could no longer serve, especially Carrickfergus. This town was of particular concern to Ward and to the commissioners due to the concentration of Presbyterians living there by the end of the century. Despite Ward's protestations, residents from both Islandmagee and Carrickfergus claimed that he had neglected his duties there for the previous two years.[9] Under Hackett and Matthews the Church of Ireland had suffered considerably and the commissioners believed that this led to the growth of Catholicism in the diocese and the influx of Presbyterian settlers from Scotland. How could the Established Church function, after all, if the structures were not in place for people to conform and attend service? Later, both Dopping and King recommended that Ward's replacement return directly to Carrickfergus (and not Lisburn as ordered by Hackett) in order to serve the town.[10]

The commissioners investigated a number of other allegations made against Ward and these concerns illustrate how one's personal fame was a central social concept in the 17th century. Perhaps the key issue for Dopping and King was that Ward was 'publickly fam'd and reported to be a person of very ill life and scandelous behaviour'.[11] Of the 22 charges brought before Ward, only two referred to his duties as a minster within the Church. The other 20 referred explicitly to his character, his behaviour and his relationship with the laity. In a desperate attempt to protect his reputation before the proceedings were issued against him, Ward, it was alleged, hastily tried to cover his tracks by encouraging illiterate people to sign a statement declaring his good character. Overall, these accusations portrayed Ward as a poor representative of the Church in the wider community. The list of offences covered a range of infractions: 10 articles accused him of adultery, five charged him with fathering an illegitimate child, while a further six claimed that he had solicited women for sexual favours. It is no surprise that three charges against Ward explicitly stated that he had a bad reputation or was of an 'ill fame' among women in his diocese. The very first article expressed that it was commonly reported that Ward 'being a person of a very incontent life & scandalous behavior is publickly fam'd and reported to be guilty of the severall notorious adulteries and other shamefull acts of lewdness and incontency [*sic*] of life'. This was a 'great dishonor of your ecclesiastical function and the notorious scandal and offence of all good Christians'.[12] In short, Ward was under examination not only for actions he was accused of but also for his reputation; he had not cultivated a reputation befitting a pious minister and so his behaviour as well as his 'public fame' were on trial.

The centrality of fame to early modern communities is reflected in the fact that Ward was allowed to challenge and investigate the public fame of his accusers as part of the proceedings in order to ascertain their credibility. Someone's hearsay testimony could be dismissed if it originated from a person of ill repute and the veracity of eyewitness testimony could be put in doubt if the deponent had dishonourable motives for testifying. At first, Ward attempted to undermine his accusers' testimonies by questioning whether and how long they knew him. Only eight of the witnesses could testify as to exactly how long they knew Ward. Some knew Ward personally as he had either served them directly as minister or because they had met him in various social settings. William Walker of Lisburn claimed that his maidservant had pointed out Ward to him as she had lived previously in Carrickfergus and knew him well.[13] This was a clear attempt by Ward to show that some people were testifying on the basis of his public fame alone. This would prove important later when Ward hoped to undermine their testimonies by claiming they were not reputable characters and thus their version of his public fame was inadmissible. The evidence people gave to prove that they did know Ward provides a fascinating window into the early modern locality. William Walker stated that after his maidservant had pointed out Ward he noted his gown and riding cap; thus, when through the cracks of a door he saw Ward lying on a bed with a woman he was sure that it was Ward from the cap and riding gown. Walker's wife also claimed to recognize Ward's gown. Of course, such testimonies were problematic and could easily be undermined. One of the Walkers' neighbours, John Johnson, informed William Walker that he had known Ward for several years and 'never knew him to ride in such a cap or in his gown'.[14] The veracity of eyewitness testimony could also be challenged by querying deponents' motivations for testifying.

Ward attempted to undermine the credibility of those who testified against him by casting aspersions on their motivations for appearing and by extension on their character. Thomas Orpin, Andrew Clements and Samuel Ward all testified that they did not witness Ward commit any of his various indiscretions, yet they were still called as witnesses to his public fame.[15] As Ward's reputation was under examination he was allowed to examine witnesses to ascertain their motivations for testifying. Thus, witnesses were asked whether they had met with Catherine Hackett, the disgraced bishop's wife, or with Mary Cole to co-ordinate their testimonies or to receive money for testifying against him. Not all were promised money by Mary Cole but Mary Nelson claimed that Cole offered to pay her travel expenses to attend the royal commission from Dublin.[16] Some complained that Ward's supporters had intimidated them in the run-up to the proceedings. Jane Wilson claimed that she was 'threatened with stoning [and] abused and called whore for swearing against him [Ward] by a company of boys in the town of Lisburne'. Ellen Walker claimed that she was afraid of incurring Ward's wrath after testifying against him. Most would later state that their true motivation for testifying at the proceedings was to see justice being served.[17] Previously, a rift had erupted among the laity and this emerged during the proceedings. Lemuel Matthews and Ward had a public falling out that dragged other members of the local community into their hotly contested dispute. Thus, Ward argued, some had testified out of loyalty to Lemuel Matthews. For example, Thomas Higginson, who testified that Ward had made a pass at his wife, collected tithes on behalf of Matthews. Ward stated that Matthews was 'known to be a capitall and mortall enemy' to him, while Higginson despised Ward because he had excommunicated Higginson's father, brother and sister for 'high misdemeanours and contempts'.[18] Lest there were any doubts about Higginson's character Ward called upon one witness to inform the commissioners that Higginson had been arraigned for murder in 1685 but was acquitted.[19] Another way in which Ward hoped to discredit the testimonies of his opponents was to argue that they were Presbyterians who sought to undermine the Established Church. In the words of Hugh Smith, most of the witnesses produced against Ward were 'rigid Presbiterians'.[20] Thus, part of the task the commissioners faced was to separate out the various factions within the world of public fame in the diocese.

As Bolton's guide for justices of the peace showed, one's character and therefore one's credibility was undermined if one had committed a criminal act. Thus, Ward asked the witnesses who testified against him to state openly whether they were guilty or defamed or reported to be guilty of any 'scandalous and notorious crimes'. Ward was, more than likely, very disappointed by the fact that all of the witnesses claimed to have a clean slate; one even carried a certificate of her good behaviour from a prominent local family.[21] Ward then called upon his supporters to comment on the credibility of his accusers both in the local community and at the proceedings. In this manner he was able to undermine the evidence presented against him by discrediting those who deposed against him and those who publicly disseminated his ill fame. The first person targeted by Ward was Margaret Higgins, who had publicly declared that she had given birth to Ward's child. William Mathey of Glenarm testified that Higgins had several illegitimate children with different fathers and this was well known among prominent people in the locality.[22] Sexual behaviour was a useful stick with which to thrash a reputation. In a similar way, the testimony of Jane Eard was undermined by the fact that she regularly slept with a local soldier and 'pretended to be married' to him. Another witness claimed that Eard was 'a notorious whore'.[23] Ward then sought to undermine the testimony of William Walker and his wife by showing the commissioners that Walker was the proprietor of a bawdy house in Lisburn. Several witnesses supported Ward's assertion on this point; one claimed that Walker's house was an ill house where 'idle loose people' were entertained and that 'Walker is of very little repute or credit amongst his neighbours'. To make matters worse, Walker was portrayed as the weaker party in his marriage after it appeared that his wife had publicly admonished him as a 'foole and a beast' for not knowing the full details of the testimony that they were going to present at the proceedings against Ward. Walker's wife, Eleanor, was also called a 'witch'.[24] While the witnesses who testified against Ward may not have been guilty of any crimes, Ward attempted to undermine their credibility by arguing that some of them had loose sexual morals and a poor character thereby casting aspersions on the reliability of their testimonies.[25]

Not all of the witnesses who testified against Ward had such questionable characters. Hugh Smith, who had earlier been described as a gentleman, testified that he paid a considerable sum of money towards the repair of the church in Islandmagee. Later, however, he was asked to testify on the credibility of his fellow deponents. While Elizabeth Berry had a 'bastard child', Smith argued Elizabeth Ross was 'an honest woman' as were Mary McComb, Catherine Spencer, Elizabeth Matthews and Isabell Browne. Jane Dawson and James Gibbons also claimed that these four women were 'honest good people'.[26] Catherine Blackburn also defended the credibility of some of her fellow witnesses and claimed that they were all 'sober good persons'; thus, she argued, their testimonies were valid.[27] It appeared that the case against Ward exacerbated tensions at a local level, particularly in Carrickfergus, Islandmagee and Lisburn. James Dorroch was called upon to verify Thomas Higginson's character and he claimed that 'he formerly looked upon him the said Higginson to be an honestman but heard since the Regall Visitacon but knows not from whome that the said Higginson was guilty of perjury'.[28] Another deponent, Randall Bruce, who served as a justice of the peace in Lisburn, believed that the Walkers were 'quiet harmless people' but ever since the proceedings were called against Ward, Bruce claimed that people began to spread rumours that they ran a brothel.[29] News of the impending proceedings against Hackett, Matthews and Ward set tongues wagging and supporters rallied behind their respective factions in the court of local opinion, which were then reflected in the proceedings.

The proceedings against Ward provide an interesting perspective on gender relations and the role of women. The use of female witnesses in legal trials slowly evolved during the medieval and early modern periods. In medieval Germany, women's words held little sway in a legal setting.[30] In the 17th century, contemporaries noted the potentially destructive nature of the female tongue in regard to public fame. It is noteworthy that many of the female witnesses who testified against Ward were subsequently discredited for their alleged loose sexual morals. Other witnesses argued that female testimony was valuable. It is also worth pointing out that many of the women whom Ward was alleged to have sexual liaisons with were either his maidservants or women of known ill repute. There are a number of ways to interpret this. On the one hand, if these allegations are true, perhaps Ward exploited well-known social divisions and believed that his position of authority meant that he could escape punishment as, due to the humble origin of these women, no one would believe their stories.[31] On the other hand, if these allegations were false and were deliberately disseminated by those who disliked Ward, they effectively portrayed him as a sexual predator. The proceedings against Ward, therefore, offer an opportunity to see the nuances in gender relations and roles in the early modern community and show the spectrum of female experiences in early modern Ireland.

While the bribery or coercion of witnesses is a well-known issue in the course of legal proceedings, this section has also shown how a person's actions in the past had a clear effect on their reputation and social credibility. Ward's attempts to defend those who testified on his behalf and to undermine those who deposed against him illustrate how central one's moral and social behaviour was in assessing the credibility of one's testimonies in a legal setting. While Ward presented little evidence that those who testified against him had been bribed or that they had colluded with one another to corroborate their testimonies, he was more successful in casting aspersions on their character by claiming that some of the witnesses were disreputable.

★ ★ ★

The dissection of witnesses' characters in the proceedings against Ward casts light on local factions, which raises the question: how exactly did public fame operate in the late 17th century? All forms of evidence provided in legal contexts had to be examined and cross-examined; thus the use of witnesses testimonies had to be justified. Ward's interrogation of the witnesses who testified both on his behalf and against him illustrated fame as a social process at a local level.[32]

Hackett's reputation had certainly preceded him when he appeared before the commissioners. Those who testified against Hackett portrayed his actions after his return to Ireland as a cynical attempt to restore his reputation and to 'remove scandal', knowing that he was under suspicion of gross neglect of his duties.[33] Hackett claimed that the negative public fame that denigrated his name 'springeth from the malice of some person or persons having noe good will to this respondent or to episcopal honour as living under some ... suspition of crimes censureable by this respondent'. Crucially, Hackett argued that the public fame about him was 'not believed true by any grave pious and good persons'.[34] Matthews, to a certain extent, also fell by the sword of his reputation.

He had already annoyed the commissioners by presenting them with a report on Church livings in the diocese that accused prominent local laymen of usurping Church revenues by fraud. The turmoil of the mid-17th century allowed many secular lords to claim lands as their own that they had never owned and thus 'diverse have gained in ye rebellious times past most of ye possessions belonging to ye said bishopric either by fraud or by force'.[35] Matthews ended his report by claiming that a total of 35 parishes had their revenues 'usurped by laymen' and claimed that he could prove the Church's title.[36]

The Established Church, however, needed the cooperation of the local laity in order to rebuild itself in the region and was unwilling to pursue Matthews' agenda. Instead, Dopping and King accused Matthews of misbehaviour and claimed that he had 'given general and great offence to very many of all degrees and ranks of persons, in the said respective diocese'.[37] It appeared that several members of the local nobility were irritated by Matthews' actions as the Lords Donegall, Longford, Massereene and Mount Alexander were all named by various witnesses as victims of Matthews' aggressive and inappropriate behaviour.[38] Not only had Matthews alienated the local laity from the Church but his fellow clergymen also felt isolated by his behaviour: 'It is generally observed and reported that Archdeacon Lemuel Matthews is of a litigious temper and practice, and that he has put several of the clergy and gentry of Downe, to a great deal of trouble and disobliged most of them.'[39] The accusation that Matthews had an aggressive character undermined his defence not only during the proceedings in 1693 but also upon his attempts at securing an appeal in 1703 when the account of proceedings against him was published anonymously. The key point was that Matthews' reputation reflected poorly not only on himself but also on the wider institution of the Church and threatened its standing among and relationship with, the laity.

Most notably Matthews had fallen out with Ward prior to the royal visitation of 1694 and Ward argued that many of the witnesses called against him were supporters of Matthews. In 1691, the two men had publicly argued during the convening of a consistorial court at Lisburn, which technically was under Ward's jurisdiction. Already, by this stage, Matthews was known as 'a litigious person and to have encouraged needless lawsuits'.[40] Matthews had tried to use consistorial courts in order to challenge the distribution of Church livings among the laity, despite being advised by his fellow clergymen not to do so. Understandably, this exacerbated tensions between Matthews and his fellow clergymen and the wider community.[41] In what appeared to be a serious error on Ward's part, he asked Matthews to perform his duties while he attended to business in England. On Ward's return to the diocese, Matthews refused to acknowledge Ward's prior jurisdiction at the consistorial court in Lisburn. The situation was already tense, but matters were not helped by the fact that Ward wished to advocate on behalf of one Mr Farrelly who had been brought before the court. Matthews denied Ward the opportunity to do so and he admonished

Ward 'thrice to hold his tongue, upon pain of excommunication'.[42] Some of the witnesses cared little about whether Matthews or Ward had law on their side but simply noted that these 'hot words' were a 'great offence to all people and rendered the jurisdiction contemptible' as the event became publicly debated among the locals.[43] Both men had brought great scandal to the Church of Ireland at a time when their position was particularly vulnerable and they should have acted in a manner befitting their position.

One could be tempted to see fame as a process that reflected an individual's local popularity. Hackett, Matthews and Ward blamed their accusers of factionalism but a closer investigation of how Ward attempted to discredit negative accounts of his behaviour illustrates that fame operated in more complex ways. On a superficial level, Ward's life was viewed by the commissioners through the lens of other people's talk and their perception of his character. The commissioners, therefore, presided over the court of local opinion as well as investigating Ward's behaviour as dean of Connor. This is not to suggest that Ward's ill fame was accepted uncritically by the laity and clergy in Down and Connor. On the contrary, as part of the proceedings against Ward, many of the witnesses outlined the way they assessed the veracity of these rumours and his public fame. For example, allegations of excessive imbibing of alcohol were particularly detrimental to the Church and the commissioners investigated whether Ward was a 'frequenter' of alehouses. Ward staunchly defended himself against these allegations and asked the commissioners whether any of their 'pretended witnesses' had heard this reported by 'grave and juditious persons'. Five witnesses admitted that they had not heard these rumours from credible people.[44]

Assessing the credibility of a disseminator of public fame was another means through which its veracity could be ascertained but there were other steps taken by contemporaries in this process, revealing the close relationship between the social order and the dissemination of public fame. Ward challenged the 'pretended witnesses' who testified against him and asked those who knew of his public fame for adultery if they had heard it from 'grave and sober persons'.[45] On this point the commissioners recorded eight witnesses' responses. Some believed that parts of Ward's reported fame were a product of local factionalism. Richard Griffith confessed that he had heard of this ill fame but had discounted its veracity because he believed the rumours had been deliberately disseminated by Presbyterians and Ward's enemies within the Church of Ireland (presumably Matthews' supporters). Archibald McNeale also reported this point as sufficient reason to discredit Ward's 'ill fame'.[46] David Maxwell, private chaplain to the earl of Mount Alexander,[47] captured the tensions that existed among the different Protestant sects at this time in his testimony as to why he did not believe Ward's ill fame. This fame 'was reported by persons whose testimony and authority this respondent laid no wait [sic] upon att hearing'. Maxwell claimed that those who spread this rumour did so out of their 'opposition' to the Established

Church and because of the 'contrarity of their perswasion in religion to the said dean'. In Maxwell's experience, 'such sort of people have reported things of the clergy of the Church of Ireland which he this respondent hath afterwards upon enquiry found to be false'.[48] Others looked at the credibility of the people who spoke negatively about Ward. Two witnesses admitted that they had heard 'grave and sober persons' speak of Ward's ill fame. One claimed that they merely reported its existence while the other claimed that they spoke of it in a 'jocular way'.[49] Thus, people assessed the credibility of the rumour by the reputation of those who spoke it and the manner in which they said it. Others attempted to compare Ward's public fame with their own personal knowledge. One witness could not reconcile Ward's reputation of an incontinent life with his public preaching against the sins of adultery, fornication and uncleanliness.[50] William Boyd, who had known Ward for at least 11 years, admitted that he had heard that Ward had a public fame of indulging in adultery but he did not believe it simply from his encounters with Ward and from observing his behaviour and conversation. Robert Hamilton succinctly captured this process when he deposed that he had heard that Ward was 'given' to women but not from 'any grave or judicious persons'. Hamilton had decided not to believe the rumours because of his 'conversation ... with the said dean'. Hamilton explained that he was reluctant to believe these rumours until he heard 'the same from good and credible witnesses'.[51] Other witnesses also revealed to the commissioners that they had employed some degree of discretion in analysing Ward's 'common fame'. For example, Elizabeth Matthews deposed that 'common fame sais ill things of dean ward' but she did not believe 'everything she hears of him, butt believe him guilty of som[e] [of] what is said of him'.[52] Mary McComb was more blunt when she informed the commissioners that she had heard a rumour that Ward had fathered an illegitimate child, 'but she believes it no further than what common fame may induce her'.[53] Another deponent, James Martin, had been solicited by Mary Cole at the 1693 harvest to testify against Ward at the proceedings. He refused to do so because he had never heard that Ward had loose sexual morals from any body but 'idle persons to whome he gave no creditt'.[54]

The key question remains, therefore, what exactly was Ward's public fame? Throughout the diocese it appeared that Ward was a man of ill repute. In Islandmagee the locals, allegedly, 'have been att varience' with Ward accused him of various sexual indiscretions. In Carrickfergus locals believed that Ward had slept with a local artisan's daughter.[55] Jane Wilson, the daughter of an innkeeper in Islandmagee, was the object of Ward's affections and 'as it is publickly fam'd and reported' Ward offered her money in return for sexual favours.[56] In Larne 'there was a publick fame' that Ward had had sexual relations with Margaret Lane.[57] In Glenarm locals reported that Ward had fathered a child with Margaret Higgins.[58] Ward denied all of these charges but the commissioners repeated their allegations that Ward's reputation across the diocese was that he was a person of 'ill life and scandelous behaviour' who frequented alehouses. Ward once again denied this and countered by claiming that his visits to alehouses only occurred 'when the duties of his calling and other lawfull occasion called him'. He further challenged the commissioners to find a witness who could testify to the fact that he had ever been excessively drunk.[59] Mary Wilson briefly supported Ward's defence, claiming he only attended alehouses 'as other gentlemen do'.[60] Despite this, Isabella Brown provided testimony that sat neatly with the evidence of Ward's accusers. Brown heard and was 'apt to believe' that Ward was a person of ill life who for 'much of [his] life has beene offensive and hath caused many to leave the church of which [she] is a member'.[61] Here, Brown captured the devastating effect of Ward's public fame. People within her community, having heard of Ward's behaviour, left the Church.

Despite the fact that Ward's relations with the local inhabitants in Islandmagee were frosty, not everybody willingly accepted the public fame that he sired illegitimate children. William Dawson decried such stories as emanating from 'severall idle persons' and thus the story should be discounted as 'he knows no ground there was for the said report'.[62] Within Carrickfergus, some were annoyed at what they perceived to be the constant rumour-mongering among the locals. John Windor complained that Mary Wilson was deliberately spreading falsehoods about her former master and told the commissioners that he was concerned for Ward's reputation and sanity. Windor had heard that Ward fell into a passion and said 'ye might as well take away my life' upon hearing of his public fame in the town.[63] Locals did not know what to believe because Wilson was neither punished for slandering Ward nor for committing fornication with him.[64] The problem was that 'credible' reports of Ward's indiscretions emerged and were believed. Isabella Brown dismissed reports that Ward had committed various acts of adultery and fornication, 'until last Winter when Betty Rose a girl of 11 years of age told her that one Mrs Gulfe had been summoned by Ward into a private chamber where the young girl (peeping through a crack in the door) saw Ward put his hands under Gulfe's clothes and used some fears wards [*sic*] to her and said he would make her husband his receiver'.[65] Despite this, Mary Torbury did not know whether to believe the public fame about Ward but she noted that 'good people are troubled at such reports'. Some believed Higgins' claims that Ward fathered her child despite her sexual indiscretions in the past. Others acknowledged Ward's ill fame but claimed that it did not fit his character.[66] For example, some quickly rejected stories that Ward had slept with Margaret Higgins because the person who spread the story, Jennet McCarty, was known as a 'scandalous person'.[67] Mary Torbury deposed that she had heard a general report of Ward's behaviour towards women but her experiences of Ward were of a man who did not have an 'unhandsome carriage'.[68] Catherine Spencer, whose integrity was defended rigorously at the end of the trial, admitted that Ward had an ill fame but believed that it was a 'scandalous report from those who bear him a grudge'; according to Spencer, Ward was a 'charetable good man'.[69] Perhaps these witnesses were loyal or sympathetic to Ward; perhaps they did not know him too well; perhaps they treated public fame with greater care than others. For the commissioners, this was a moot point. Ward should have behaved in such a way as to avoid any suspicion of these infractions.

The commissioners had to wade through local grudges, clerical rivalries, and the court of public opinion in their investigations into Ward as dean of Connor. They had to carefully pick their way through the testimonies of a range of people from various social strata who provided evidence that Ward was either an upstanding member of the community or an immoral character. The proceedings captured the range of views on Ward's reputation and it appeared that, to some extent, there was a public fame that Ward led an immoral life. Not all accepted this uncritically. Ward had allies and opponents among the laity and the clergy; some, who did not know Ward personally, assessed his fame by employing a range of processes that reflected contemporary values invested in the social order, sexual politics and public behaviour. Not only did public fame capture what happened in a local community, it also recorded the credibility of individual members. It was to be a key component in all of the proceedings orchestrated by Dopping and King. Nonetheless, it became clear to the commissioners that they had to ascertain whether Ward was guilty of the various crimes of a sexual nature that he was accused of, as his public fame could only hint at his guilt.

3. Sex and society in east Ulster

Having established the centrality of *fama* or common fame to early modern local societies it is necessary to focus on the central thrust of Dean Ward's trial. Aside from neglecting his position as dean of Connor, Ward was also accused of several sexual infractions and of fathering a number of illegitimate children. These accusations, however, were exceedingly difficult to prove without the actual testimonies of those who engaged in these activities with Ward and they raise a whole number of questions such as: how did one 'prove' the paternity of an illegitimate child in the 17th century? How can one 'prove' that an adulterous liaison has taken place? Understandably, witnesses to such crimes were few and far between (or unlikely to step forward). Thus, it is necessary to establish how the commissioners ascertained Ward's guilt. This process reveals how local societies understood infractions of a sexual nature and the different social elements that could be drawn upon to determine guilt.

★ ★ ★

Illegitimacy affected the moral, political and social world in which Ward lived. At the level of political discourse, illegitimacy reflected and defined the course of colonial politics in Ireland. Hostile English commentators, steeped in traditions of primogeniture, commented caustically on Irish heredity laws that allowed an illegitimate son to succeed to his father's title. This could prove problematic to those used to English customs. Thus, they called for the greater implementation of English common law to prevent this practice among certain sections of Irish society. Therefore, English colonial treatises on Ireland viewed the practices of bastardy within Irish society as another example of Irish primitiveness. At a local level, the labels 'illegitimate' or 'bastard' were used to denigrate and insult a rival. These terms did not simply imply that the child's mother had loose sexual morals, they also informed the victim of their relegated status as a sub-category in local society and their disgrace to the community's collective piety. There is little evidence available from which one can draw concrete conclusions about the prevalence of illegitimate births during this period. By the 18th and 19th centuries, however, it has been estimated that 2.5 per cent of all live births in Ireland were illegitimate.[1] As is often the case, historians of the 17th century are left to ponder fragmentary evidence, such as that presented by Ward's trial, and wonder how reflective it was of wider social trends.

Contemporaries certainly believed that illegitimacy was a widespread issue across Europe. Cyclical bouts of hysteria claimed that unmarried pregnant women hid their condition (and, by extension, their immoral sexual behaviour) from their peers. Thus, adultery, fornication and bastardy appeared to be a widespread problem that occurred daily, beyond the observance of the local community. To complete the act of concealment, it was alleged that unmarried mothers-to-be later abandoned or killed their newborn child in the hope that they could maintain a veneer of chastity and secure a successful marriage in the future. In truth, however, the all-seeing eye of local communities, such as those in east Ulster where Ward lived, meant that this was quite difficult. While flight was an option for pregnant single women, a recent study has shown that for the most part single mothers in early modern Scotland rarely took this option. Instead they accepted the disciplinary procedures of society and the Church, and gave birth to their illegitimate child.[2] On the one hand, there was clearly a social stigma attached to illegitimacy in Ireland as many English Protestant settlers claimed to have been denounced as 'English bastard' or 'Protestant bastard' during the 1641 rebellion.[3] Furthermore, at the turn of the 18th century, it was alleged that members of the Church of Ireland called Presbyterian children 'bastards and sons of whores' because they did not recognize the validity of Presbyterian marriages.[4] On the other hand evidence from the mid-17th century suggests that many people were able to identify the illegitimate children of prominent members of the local community, suggesting a degree of normality about the practice. Peter Laslett has argued that a subculture of bastardy and sexual non-conformity existed in the early modern period but this theory has not met with universal acceptance.[5] What can be argued is that, while illegitimacy may have been discouraged by clerical and secular leaders and led to bouts of social hysteria, it remained a visible part of life in the late 17th century.

Although Dean Ward had been married and was a widower by the time of his trial, he was nonetheless accused of fathering a number of illegitimate children. It is not clear from the record that has survived as to whether these illicit unions occurred before or after Ward's wife had died. Either way, these accusations demonized Ward's character and brought scandal upon his local community and the Church. Ward denied fathering any illegitimate children and the prosecution took a number of steps to prove his guilt. The early modern equivalent of a paternity test could only focus on what could be observed within the local community. Thus, one of the ways in which paternity was ascertained was through an investigation into whether those accused of fathering an illegitimate child exhibited the sort of behaviour society expected of them. For example, as part of the third charge put before him, Ward was accused of fathering Ann Wilson's child and 17 witnesses attested to the local belief of Ward's paternity. Some alleged that Ward contributed financially to the child's upbringing. This was one way paternity could be inferred. If a man paid money to a woman who was not his wife for the support of her child, so the argument went, surely he did so because of his moral responsibility as a father? Two people testified that Ward paid maintenance to Ann Wilson and they outlined the mechanics as to how this money was raised. Jane McKenly claimed that her first husband, Thomas Dawson, collected the Easter offerings and book money in Carrickfergus. Ward instructed Dawson, McKenly alleged, to give some of these monies to Ann Wilson. Andrew Clements, a local doctor, claimed that Ward also ordered him to give money to Ann Wilson. In total, Clements estimated that he had given her £10 at Ward's behest.[6] William and Elizabeth Dawson later claimed that they reared another one of Ward's illegitimate children and that they had been paid, on Ward's instructions, out of the local tithes.[7] Not all of Ward's alleged illegitimate offspring were so lucky, however. Ward was supposed to have paid the princely sum of £15 maintenance to Margaret Higgins per quarter and a once-off payment of 6s. after she had borne him an illegitimate child. Several other witnesses stated that the sums Ward actually paid to Higgins were considerably smaller. Robert McGomery, for example, heard that Ward paid Higgins 14d. per quarter. Allegedly, Higgins and Ward quarreled over these payments. Higgins complained that she was in great want of money. In order to shame Ward into fulfilling his moral responsibilities (as a father, not a minister), Higgins threatened to leave the child on Ward's doorstep.[8]

While discouraging adultery, fornication and sexual intercourse outside of marriage, most legal codes outlined provisions for illegitimate children and accepted the fact that illegitimate children needed financial support. Brehon law, for example, deemed the maintenance of children outside of marriage as the sole responsibility of the father. If a man impregnated another man's wife, or a servant or slave, or if he raped somebody, he had sole responsibility for paying for the child.[9] In 1520, Galway Corporation issued a decree stating that any man who impregnated a woman either had to marry her or 'gyve hir such goodes as shall be lawfull towards hir preferment until another maie [marry her]'.[10] In Irish common law, fathers were obligated to support their illegitimate offspring financially, otherwise the local parish had to bear the cost.[11] Such attitudes informed and reflected 17th-century Irish social values and it is clear that the prosecution hoped to show that the payments by Ward to unmarried mothers to assist with the rearing of their illegitimate children were a sign that he was, in fact, their father. The payment of maintenance alone did not, however, suffice as proof of paternity. As one witness testified, some people believed that Ward did this 'out of charity'.[12] Thus, the prosecution had to rely on a number of other ways by which paternity could be established, as it could readily be inferred that Ward simply followed the rules and paid for the upkeep of these illegitimate children out of the parish coffers, as outlined in various legal codes in Ireland.

A number of midwives also testified in cases like this where they could play a role in proving paternity in the early modern period. Contemporary explanations of a midwife's duties connected their practical purpose with wider religious and social responsibilities. Extant medical reference books outlined

the ideal characteristics a midwife should have. In 1670, an English doctor based
in Cork, James Wolveridge, published *Speculum matricis: or the expert midwives'*
handmaid. While he deliberately chose to publish the book in English (not Latin)
and in London to serve English midwives he did hope that 'it may be serviceable'
to Irish midwives also. Wolveridge, using appropriate references from the Old
Testament book of Exodus, argued that midwives needed good memories,
and should be kind, slow to anger, literate, studious and knowledgeable of the
'female condition'. Their moral obligation was to 'fear God'.[13] Other extant
guides on midwifery also expressed the need for midwives to have an upright
moral character and pleasant disposition.[14] Aside from delivering children,
midwives also had a moral duty to perform. In some cases they had to ensure
the mother of an illegitimate child swore an oath not to abandon her offspring
afterwards. In England, for example, while in labour women had to swear
'that the childe should stick to me as the barke to the tree'.[15] When unmarried
mothers went into labour, midwives were also supposed to ascertain the identity
of the child's father. If the pregnant woman refused to cooperate midwives
could withdraw their support. This may have been in deference to their moral
compass or because of financial considerations. When in 1688 Eleanor Wall
presented herself before Ann Whiterly, a Drogheda midwife, and declined to
tell Whiterly who the father of the child was, Whiterly refused to assist Wall
in her labour. Wall, in what was probably a desperate attempt for help, assured
the midwife that she would be paid.[16] Furthermore, midwives were expected to
furnish the identity of an illegitimate child's father so that he, and not the local
parish coffers, would support the child financially.[17] Thus, midwives were often
called upon to establish paternity.[18]

Some of the midwives who allegedly delivered Ward's illegitimate children
claimed that they had fulfilled their moral obligations in performing this
particular act (or wanted the Church authorities to think that they had fulfilled
this function). This language of pious duty no doubt reflected their surroundings
in an ecclesiastical court. In one instance, Elizabeth Chapman deposed that
when Margaret Higgins came to her house in the middle of labour she refused
to help Higgins until she admitted the child's paternity; Higgins thus declared
that it was Ward's child and delivered a daughter after much trouble.[19] Some
of those midwives who helped Ward's alleged pregnant mistresses still assisted
them despite their refusal to co-operate in naming the father of the child.[20]
When Ann Townley asked Judith Beaker for help in delivering a child, Beaker
did not ask about the child's paternity as Townley was married. Beaker later
heard that Ward, not Townley's husband, was rumoured to be the child's father.
So Beaker later performed her duty and inquired about the father's identity.[21]
Such testimony, which offered the reported speech of those implicated in
court, was common. In England, for example, a murder victim's dying words
– in which they identified their killer – was often enough evidence to convict
the murderer.[22] In both moments it was believed that it was impossible for

the speaker to tell a lie. Thus, the declarations of women mid-labour as to the paternity of their child were considered to be of value as evidence in these cases, once credible witnesses reported them.

None of the women who, allegedly, gave birth to Ward's children testified during his trial so the prosecution provided only hearsay testimony on Ward's paternity of several illegitimate children. Those who could testify that they had heard Ward's various mistresses claim he fathered their child were called upon. For example, Margaret Cole heard Margaret Daly confess that Ward fathered her baby, who subsequently died.[23] Hearsay evidence on this point was obviously problematic as a further two witnesses cast doubts on Ward's paternity of Daly's deceased child.[24] As discussed previously, however, Ward was also being judged on his reputation; thus, much of the evidence brought forth about his paternity of several illegitimate children indicated that the wider community believed he had fathered these children. Andrew Clements testified that there was a 'common fame' that Ann Wilson's child, Betty, was 'a child of the Dean Ward's gott on ye body of the said Ann Wilson'; which was confirmed by 12 other witnesses.[25] Similarly, Robert Donnell deposed that common fame stated that Ward had fathered a child with Catherine Magee, while Mary Torbury said that she 'never heard of one Catherine Magee who had any child to deane Ward but heard of one Allice Magee who bore a child to him'.[26] When Agnus Glascow was called upon to testify about Ward's sexual relations with Margaret Higgins, Glascow claimed that everybody believed Ward had fathered Higgins' child and 'that the fame of itt is and has bin notorious and nott contradicted thro ye whole country'.[27] Likewise, there was a 'report' that Ward had sent one of his 'bastard children' to be cared for at the house of Samuel Baker and then Matthew Logan in Islandmagee. In this particular instance the child's nurse testified that 'it was reported that the said Dean [Ward] was the father of the said child'.[28] Not all, of course, believed these rumours. Catherine Spencer upon hearing Jennet McCarthy's gossip that Ward was the father of an illegitimate child, declared that 'ye said Jennet was a scandelous naughty husey not fitt to be beliv'd'.[29] Despite the presentation of this contradictory evidence to the court, piece-by-piece the prosecution hoped to establish Ward's paternity of these children based on Ward's fame and other factors. First, they argued that he maintained these illegitimate children not out of charity but out of his paternal responsibilities. Second, they called upon midwives who performed their moral obligation and demanded the name of the father from unmarried women in labour. Third, they established that many people believed Ward was the father and that there was some substance to this 'fame'. Finally, they turned to another key element, the names and hereditary traits of Ward's alleged children.

Sometimes, nomenclature could indicate the paternity of a bastard child. Margaret Higgins named her daughter Mary Ward in homage to the child's father.[30] Higgins had earlier attempted to protect Ward's reputation at the Presbyterian sessions when she was tried for adultery. Higgins explained that she was not guilty of adultery but fornication as Mary's father was a widower. She asked the sessions not to publicize Ward's name after she had declared his paternity. Higgins' concern for Ward's reputation clearly dissipated when he proved reluctant to provide financial assistance for the rearing of the child.[31] Mary Ward, however, was not an only child, nor was she the only illegitimate child that Mary Higgins gave birth to. Ward thus attempted to undermine Higgins as a credible witness by revealing to the court that Higgins also had a son born outside of wedlock. Thus, Higgins' loose sexual morals reflected poorly on her character and her credibility as a witness.[32] Matters were further complicated when Higgins was unsure who the father of her son was. At the Presbyterian sessions, she claimed that it could be Simon Beard. There was a common fame, however, that Cornelius Cowan was actually the father. In order to deal with this contested paternity, the 'country people' called Higgins' son Simon Cornelius 'after both the fathers', thereby illustrating the common practice of naming illegitimate children after their father (and perhaps also revealing how limited this practice was as a means of indicating paternity).[33] The naming of a child after a father may have been done to shame them into providing greater financial support for the mother and child. When, in 1687, David Keefe refused to care dutifully for his illegitimate son, Elizabeth Darby (Keefe's former mistress) called the child David to remind him of his responsibilities.[34] Naming practices were not the only indicator of paternity. While Ann Wilson called her daughter Elizabeth or Betty Ward in order to indicate that Ward was indeed the father of the child, Thomas Orpin further testified that Elizabeth was 'very like Dean Ward'.[35] Orpin's remark that the child was like her father was an important distinction to make in a legal context. In Gaelic society a child's appearance, manner and gestures could be used to indicate paternity in brehon law courts. According to brehon tradition, if a woman had slept with two different men and did not know who the father of her child was, then the child was to be left alone for three years 'till the kin-appearance, kin-voice, and kin-manners come to him ... whichever of the two men he takes after ... the child is the offspring of the man whom he resembles more'.[36] While Irish common law commentaries did not provide great detail on this particular subject, the attitude captured in brehon legal texts was very similar to what was practiced in this case at least, and was probably shared in Irish common law and Church of Ireland courts. The early modern world, therefore, called upon a number of different approaches to establish paternity that included physical appearance but also common knowledge, declarations by unmarried mothers in labour and the payment of child maintenance.

* * *

Ward was also accused of a number of sexual indiscretions and of attempted sexual assaults. The definition of rape was clear in Sir Richard Bolton's guide for justices of the peace, but sexual assault was less clearly defined, as was adultery and fornication. Contemporaries recognized the difficulties authorities faced when prosecuting crimes of a sexual nature. As Henry Jones, the dean of Kilmore, commented in 1643, 'wickedness of that nature have com[m] only not witnesses'. Matters were further complicated by the fact that if a woman was raped it was perceived to be a poor reflection on her 'friends and kindred'. The rape of a woman was regarded as a crime against her guardian, be it father, husband or head of kin. The nature of the crime involved a public denouncement of the rapist. This involved an admission of sexual intercourse, which constituted a stain on the woman's family's honour and status as the male members of her family had failed to protect her. All of this, Jones argued, 'forbids an indiscreet publication' if a rape victim wished to pursue a prosecution. Thus many 'have proved very tender in touching on such reports'.[37] In this instance Jones wrote about the nature of violence that erupted in Ireland after the outbreak of the Irish rebellion of 1641, but his point regarding the difficulty in reporting and prosecuting sexual violence also rang true in times of peace. The issue of consent was obviously crucial to any prosecution for rape and Bolton outlined the indicators of non-consensual sex in *A justice of the peace for Ireland*. He advised local justices of the peace that a woman should raise hue and cry if they have been raped or 'complaine thereof presently to some credible persons'. Even if a woman subsequently decided that she had consented to the act, the crime was still considered to be a rape and therefore a felony. Likewise, if a woman was threatened with death or duress and she consented as a result, this still constituted rape. The only evidence that could exonerate an alleged rapist, according to Bolton, was if a child was conceived as a result of the act. 'This is no rape', Bolton wrote, 'for a woman cannot conceive with childe, except she doe consent'. This view was not shared in early modern Irish legal tracts that accepted conception could occur as a result of a rape.[38] Like paternity, whether a rape occurred could only be established by the behaviour exhibited by the victim after the fact. She was expected to behave in certain ways and such behaviour indicated to the community that such a crime had occurred. While Bolton made no attempt to define a sexual assault or provide clues as to how adultery or fornication could be prosecuted, Ward was charged with these crimes. A number of witnesses came forward and testified to Ward's attempted sexual assaults and seductions as well as his sexual indiscretions but again these infractions left no discernible 'proof' to wider society other than the behaviour of the victims immediately afterward and their word as evidence, which depended on their credibility, fame and social status.

The sixth article charged Ward with threatening Marian Berry that he would lie with her daughter, Jennet, unless she found him another woman to satisfy his desires. Jennet took to the stand and deposed that 15 or 16 years previously she lived with her mother. Ward, she alleged, came to the house and requested brandy from Berry. When Ward saw Jennet he solicited her for sex. She declined and offered to call upon one Margaret McLane, 'who would be fitter for him'. McLane duly arrived with her child (Ward, it was alleged, offered the child a box of tobacco to play with as a distraction while he lay with McLane) and the two went upstairs. Then Jennet claimed that while she prepared dinner her brother looked through a hole in the door and saw the two in an act of 'uncleanliness'.[39] In order to demonize Ward fully, he was presented in the proceedings as a sexual predator with no regard for social mores. The eighth charge against Ward was that he had made 'vile attempts' on the chastity of three other women. Thomas Higgins testified that Ward offered his wife a guinea if she would sleep with him. Ward claimed he was only testing the woman's virtue, but his unconvinced hosts turned on him and asked how a man of his 'gown' who had just administered the sacrament could act in such a fashion. Ward, Higgins alleged, never returned to their house. Margaret Davis testified that her husband was offered a gelding worth £10 if he would allow Ward to sleep with her but she (not her husband) refused the offer.[40] Piece by piece a negative picture of Ward's character as a man with predatory sexual instincts and an insatiable sexual desire emerged.

Others were not so fortunate as to escape with an indecent proposal of a gelding or money from Ward in return for sexual favours. For example, Mary Wilson testified that while she worked as a servant in the house of the earl of Donegall in Carrickfergus, Ward 'attempted her chastity' as she carried a pail of milk on her head. Wilson was forced to throw the pail to the ground and run away.[41] Although she did not testify, evidence was presented on Mary Cole's behalf by Catherine Blackburn who claimed to have seen several bruises on her legs; these were taken to be a sign of her struggle to escape from Ward's clutches.[42] Another witness, Mary Nelson, testified that Ward had solicited his servant for sex in his wife's absence. The servant, Elizabeth Newton, had related to Nelson an incident that occurred in the early 1680s when Ward asked her to sleep with him. Ward, according to Nelson, kept 'kissing of [Newton] and putting his hands on her breasts'. Newton refused his advances. Thus, Ward looked into his closet, took out some money and threw it down Newton's chest. Newton was unsure as to whether this money was her wages or another attempt by Ward to solicit sex. Ward, in an attempt to get his way, took a bible nearby and swore an oath that his hands would only touch Newton's breasts 'and not below her girdle' if she acquiesced to his demands. Newton, Nelson claimed, played for time and relented to Ward's demands on the condition that she could call upon a friend first. Newton departed and confided to Nelson who advised that 'an ill promise was better broke[n] th[a]n kept' and thus Nelson escorted Newton back to Ward's house and the matter came to an end.[43] These women were the unfortunate victims of Ward's lust. Their testimonies about the behaviour of the clergyman were the only evidence presented on this matter. His position as a Church of Ireland dean underlined his social and moral authority, thus they probably were reluctant to raise the necessary 'hue and cry' about an attempted sexual assault for fear no one would believe them.

Ward was also accused of having consensual sex with a number of women. Pre- or extra-martial sexual intercourse required some degree of discretion and/ or the facilitation of the wider community if one were to avoid prosecution; therefore, it was unlikely that trysts outside of marriage were as prevalent as was believed. Nevertheless, this raises an interesting issue about how frequently adultery and fornication occurred in Irish society during the 17th century. Both were expressly banned in Ireland in 1612 by English legislation that took force in Ireland under Poynings' Law.[44] In the early seventeeth century, a hostile report on the Irish Catholic Church suggested that both practices were rife among Irish Catholics and claimed that the papacy accrued significant sums from 'papists' paying penance fines for sins such as drunkenness, adultery, fornication and incest. These allegedly amounted to £20,000.[45] This estimate is littered with difficulties; first, it is obviously hostile; second, all these sins were lumped into one category; and finally, it provides no exact clue as to how common a practice adultery and fornication were other than to suggest it was widespread among Irish Catholics. Cromwellian authorities were sufficiently alarmed by the lack of godly behaviour in Ireland by 1659 that they ordered for the greater implementation of laws governing drunkenness, adultery, incest and fornication.[46] In reality, various crises, presented as a punishment from God, prompted much introspection and condemnation of sinful practices such as adultery and fornication as a means to address the situation in the early modern period.

The first witness to testify to Ward's adultery was Baptist Boyd, a merchant from Carrickfergus. Boyd alleged that one night he saw Ward go into Thomas Gerdan's house. Ward, Boyd alleged, proceeded to go to bed with Gerdan's wife (which he saw through the window). Boyd then 'heard the said deane make some nois[e] w[i]th her and they thrust in what case that stopd the window over their heads on the bed whereon they lay'.[47] The third charge against Ward was that he had committed adultery with Adam Tennison's wife and was caught in the act, although the surviving record does not document the details.[48]

It may be worthwhile to consider contemporary attitudes towards sexual relations outside the marital bed and before marriage. While many members of the elite routinely maintained mistresses, such practices were frowned upon in public discourse. Furthermore, the evidence for sexual relations among the lower social orders is limited to inferences and generalizations, thus it is highly problematic to ascertain how widespread a practice it was. Take, for example, Charles Leslie's *Letter of advice to a friend* published in 1696. Leslie, a former chancellor of the cathedral of Connor, became well known for criticizing the Church of Ireland hierarchy. In this pamphlet Leslie hinted that attitudes toward adultery, fornication and polygamy were changing. 'The discourse', Leslie wrote, 'which happened in our company last night has obliged me to write this'. This pamphlet provided evidence from Scripture that fornication and adultery were not, contrary to emerging popular opinion, tolerated in the Gospel.

Those who believed their own interpretation on this matter were 'bent to their own destruction'.[49] Similarly, Dudley Loftus, an Oriental scholar and MP for Bannow, Co. Wexford, praised women for remaining chaste and chastized those who were 'pretenders onely to chastity [and have] sold their virginities as often as new made Priests do their first Mass'. Loftus spoke here of the twin evils that he believed Irish Protestant society faced in the late 17th century – popery and women with loose sexual morals. This illustrates how sexual behaviour or perceived sexual behaviour was a convenient means to denigrate rivals but also reflects wider concerns about loose sexual morals.[50]

It was also commonly believed that women who partook in sex before, or outside, marriage brought shame and dishonor to their families.[51] Thus, printed books such as *Discourses useful for the vain modish ladies and their gallants* by Francis Boyle, Viscount Shannon, an English moralist, outlined the subjugate role women had to perform. Boyle argued that romantic love and a virtuous woman were the basis of a good marriage. His description of how women should behave reveals a lot about early modern Irish society. He divided women into two groups, the first consisting of virtuous women. The second group, Boyle argued, were a 'sort of beastly Women' who 'take upon them the vile employment of common censuring, and publick rayling at all strict Vertuous Women'. These women cast aspersions on the reputation of virtuous women 'by all the ill reports they can invent'. The key difference between the two groups was that 'a pious woman sins against her will, a wicked woman with it'. Boyle was concerned at what he perceived to be the rise of women's power in the late 17th century. He claimed that there were only a few men in the kingdom of Ireland who 'govern their wives'. These concerns related specifically to contemporary fears that traditional values were being undermined.[52] It is no surprise that in a patriarchal society attitudes toward female social and political influence would be condemnatory.

By focusing on Ward's alleged sexual indiscretions, he was presented as a man unworthy of his office – a man without the esteem due to a minister of the Church of Ireland. While John Atherton is a well-known example of a cleric who brought shame to the Church of Ireland in the late 1630s, in truth the sexual behaviour of clergymen was a concern among Church hierarchies across all faiths in the 17th century. Clergymen of all denominations, unsurprisingly, were supposed to offer a good example to their flocks. In the 1650s, Colonel John Jones reminded his colleague, Colonel Robert Phayre, the governor of Cork, that a local clergyman had dishonoured 'God ... by living in the known sin of adultery'. This very issue, Jones believed, not only affected Phayre's credit but also Phayre's family and the wider community: 'The Lord grant that your poor wife and little babes may not smart and have cause to mourn bitterly for your compliance with ... those that trample upon the everlasting gospel of the Lord Jesus.'[53] William King was particularly concerned in 1694 about the calibre of men serving as ministers. He wrote to an unknown correspondent that, of

150 ministers brought before the Dublin authorities, only two or three were 'conformable' the rest were either Presbyterian, or guilty of the sins of adultery, incest or fornication.[54] Clergymen's behaviour was supposed not only to reflect the morality of the church they represented but also the piety of their flocks.

On a number of occasions witnesses expressed shock that their local minister could behave in such a manner. They believed Ward betrayed his office by his seemingly predatory attacks and his attempts to solicit sexual relations from willing accomplices. On one occasion, it was alleged, Ward was caught in an 'act of vileness' with an unnamed woman in a tavern on Fleet Street in London. Ward countered that they were not engaged in a 'vile' act but that she was, in fact, a pickpocket who had stolen several guineas from his pocket. When caught red-handed for this crime Ward at first pretended to be a different clergyman, John McNeal, the neighbouring dean of Down. Charitably, McNeal would later testify on Ward's behalf.[55] Thomas Higgins claimed that Ward visited his alehouse and called for a room and a drink. Ward then brought an unknown woman into the room with him. Higgins checked on the pair and found the door shut, but looking through a gap in the door saw Ward 'on the body of the said woman between her legs and moving in the act of uncleanness'; Higgins' wife corroborated this.[56] Ellen Walker also claimed that, through a hole in a door, she saw Ward in a compromising position with Jane Ramsey. Ward, Walker claimed, was 'upon the body of Jane Ramsey' but had covered his gown over her. As Walker was unsure whether Ward 'acted uncleanness' or not she called upon her husband to confirm. William Walker, taking to the stand, offered equally imprecise testimony. As Ward had covered their bodies with his gown, Walker was unable to confirm whether he witnessed Ward in the act of fornication.[57] The Walkers' inability to confirm whether Ward was engaged in sexual intercourse revealed the problem facing contemporaries of providing witnesses to acts of a sexual nature. The Walkers were vague on the details, and the language used to describe sexual acts was equally vague and euphemistic. As Ward was tried before members of the hierarchy of the Church of Ireland one could be tempted to assume that this was a nod to their presence. It may, therefore, have been indicative of early modern sensibilities about discussing sexual relations in formal contexts.

★ ★ ★

As noted by Henry Jones, and as can be evidenced from Irish common law and brehon law texts, the prosecution of crimes of a sexual nature was exceedingly difficult. To make matters worse, social hierarchies came into play as the testimony of women from less-respectable backgrounds or of humble origins was normally trumped by the attestations of men from the higher social echelons. It is necessary to remember, however, that Ward was prosecuted not only for the crime of adultery and fornication but also for having the reputation of an adulterer and fornicator. Ward was regularly accused of being in compromising positions. Many believed Ward was a frequent visitor to houses of ill repute to see women of loose sexual morals. This case, therefore, reveals much about the realities of sexual experiences and social anxieties in early modern Ulster. The number of illegitimate children living in east Ulster, as alluded to during Ward's trial, suggests that they were a noticeable part of the population. Clearly, sexual relations occurred outside and before marriage but it is impossible from the surviving evidence to know how prevalent these practices were. What can be inferred are the social attitudes towards such practices. People shook their heads in disapproval but they also recognized it as a fact of life. We do not know if Simon Cornelius was so called as a joke, or whether his name simply referred to his contested paternity. Furthermore, the financial provision for illegitimate children across the various legal codes suggests that early modern Irish society had adapted to the needs of illegitimate children and grudgingly provided assistance out of local coffers. Above all, Ward's trial and the testimonies about his behaviour show the sexual tribulations of our early modern counterparts and how they could portray such acts as an abuse of power by a man in a position of authority. To further compound matters, as Ward was a minister, he should have known better in the eyes of some of his clerical colleagues and members of his congregation. Despite the construction of this narrative of Ward's behaviour it is possible that Ward was the unfortunate victim of a smear campaign that coincided with a wider agenda within the Church of Ireland – namely, the consolidation of the Established Church in Ireland in the face of the burgeoning Presbyterian church.

Conclusion

A brief summary of the proceedings of Anthony Dopping and William King in the 1694 commission recorded that Thomas Ward was deprived of his office for adultery and incontinency of life. He joined Thomas Hackett and Lemuel Matthews and a number of other clergy from the diocese who were also deprived of their livings. William Milne was stripped of the prebend of Kilroot parish (where Richard Dobbs' family lived), but was granted a pension of £20 per annum because of his 'great age & poverty'. For those local parishioners who felt that Milne escaped sanction, he was 'publickly admonished' for his behaviour. The Church hierarchy was eager to reproach corrupt and nefarious ministers publicly in order to restore the reputation of the Church in the diocese, hence their investigations into clerics' reputations. The proceedings against Thomas Jones, the treasurer of Connor, further revealed the role that fame played in legal contexts and within the Church. At first, Jones was under suspicion for simony but was exonerated by the testimonies of upstanding members of the local community. After one of Jones' curates, Mr Ogilby, committed suicide it transpired that Jones, much like Matthews, had regularly underpaid his subordinates. Ogilby as a result 'laboured under soe great necessity yt out of a melancholy consideracon of his hard circumstances made himselfe away & became felo de te'; thus, Jones was removed. The commissioners also investigated whether Philip Matthews, Lemuel's nephew, was guilty of fornicating with Mary Matthews, his uncle's housekeeper. Only one witness who was a 'person of noe good fame' provided evidence for this and the charges were dropped. Similarly, the charges against David Maxwell for simony were dropped after Lemuel Matthews was convicted, as his testimony on this point was now rendered invalid because of his past behaviour, which became a key part of his fame.[1]

Public fame was a central concept in early modern society. It shaped communal discourse and helped to determine the validity of evidence presented in legal settings. The testimonies of both men and women were scrutinized during the proceedings against Thomas Ward when it came to determining his public fame. Here, women as well as men determined and represented one's local standing and reputation in the eyes of the local community. Women's testimonies were heard as part of these proceedings as the commissioners determined whether Ward had an ill fame. Certain statements could be discredited and disregarded if the deponent's character or previous behaviour lacked credibility. It is noteworthy that the aspersions cast upon those who testified against Ward were divided along gendered lines. Women who spoke ill of Ward were frequently accused of having loose sexual morals while men were either accused of committing various crimes or, as was the case with William Walker, of being subservient to their wives. At the same time, public fame was a product of local talk and therefore was subject to local factionalism and rivalry. Thus, Dopping and King had to sift through and unpack the dispute between local Presbyterian and Church of Ireland Protestant communities as well as the consequences of the public argument between Matthews and Ward in Lisburn church. Ward's alleged sexual indiscretions with female parishioners undoubtedly left some of the laity disenchanted with the Established Church.

Ward's deprivation of his office for adultery represented an attempt by the commissioners to restore the reputation of the Church in the diocese. The proceedings established that a considerable number of people in the diocese believed that Ward was guilty of adultery, fornication and of fathering a number of illegitimate children. In order to prove that Ward was guilty of fathering a number of illegitimate children the testimonies of those who had observed Ward's actions in the community were included. Public fame recorded social behaviour and the reporting of such behaviour could be used to prove infraction, such as adultery and fornication, had occurred. Allegedly, Ward kept company with women of ill repute, cavorted with women in private bedrooms, and catered for the financial welfare of his reputed children. The proceedings against Ward recorded what the eyes of the local community had observed, and what the words of local talk had reported, in the years leading up to the royal commission and visitation in 1694. Thus, Dopping's and King's investigation into a range of sexual crimes in the proceedings against Ward provides a unique insight into the early modern community and local talk.

The record that emerged from the visitation of 1694 and the proceedings against Hackett, Matthews and Ward revealed how poorly administered the Church of Ireland was in the diocese of Down and Connor. Matthews recognized this and worked to challenge the usurpation of Church livings by members of the laity in order to improve revenues and to restore the Established Church's influence. This policy did not receive official sanction or support from his colleagues as the Established Church was so vulnerable in the diocese and therefore needed the support of the laity in order to thrive. All three proceedings revealed that age-old problems of pluralism, simony and non-residency remained. Matthews' arguments that his non-residency was not his fault and that the diocese was unattractive to members of the clergy because they had no access to glebe lands, and therefore could not earn a living in their respective parishes, had a certain ring of truth to it.[2] Coupled with these structural problems, the diocese had to contend with the fact that both Hackett and Ward appeared as men ill-fitted to their function and as poor role models for the local community. They were poor representatives of the Church and the proceedings were very much an attempt to restore public confidence and a late bid to secure the conformity of Catholics and Presbyterians in the region. Over the course of the 17th century, east Ulster became an area full of multi-religious communities. Richard Dobbs' account revealed the extent of popular devotion to St Patrick and to more local religious shrines. In light of the weakness of the Church and the strength of popular religious practices the commissioners readily believed that they stood to lose significant numbers to rival churches if they did not act appropriately and swiftly. In an era that witnessed the passing of the first series of penal laws the reality of the Established Church's position in east Ulster contrasted sharply with the rhetorical triumph that followed the Williamite victory. The public movement that sought to reform the manners and behaviour of the laity reflected wider concerns with the plight of Irish Protestantism after its seeming deliverance from a popish menace in the recent past.

Ward's world, therefore, revolved around the local community that he was supposed to serve. A trace of what they spoke about has survived because of Ward's alleged behaviour and sexual infractions with members of the laity. An interesting picture of a poorly funded church in an area of considerable cosmopolitanism emerges from his proceedings, as well as of a society that accepted that behaviour deemed immoral was a part and parcel of daily life. Tensions between Church of Ireland Protestants and Presbyterians were reflected in the calling of the latter 'bastards' by the former, but the cooperation of the Presbyterian laity with Church of Ireland authorities suggests that not all relations were hostile. Furthermore, the treatment and support of illegitimate children reflected the reality that society had to cater for them if their fathers did not take responsibility. In an era of concern over the growth of female influence in Irish society an alternative picture of gender relations contrast with what was described in contemporary print.[3] Despite this, age-old insults of a sexual nature were commonly employed to denigrate females who encroached upon male spheres of influence. Finally, it is worth noting that Ward died in 1695, a year after he was deprived of his office and the same year in which two of his children were baptized into the Church of Ireland. Despite his ill reputation among women in the diocese, Ward had married again, showing that his social world did not end after his deprivation nor did his ill fame for adultery, fornication and fathering illegitimate children scupper his chances of remarrying. One is left to wonder whether, he would have contested the decision like Matthews, had he lived.

Notes

ABBREVIATIONS

BL   British Library
CSPI   *Calendar of State Papers Ireland*
DIB   *Dictionary of Irish biography* online edition
NAI   National Archives of Ireland
ODNB   *Oxford dictionary of national biography* online edition
RCBL   Representative Church Body Library
TCD   Trinity College, Dublin

INTRODUCTION

1   Henry Cotton, *Fasti ecclesiae hibernicae: the succession of the prelates and members of the cathedral bodies of Ireland* (5 vols, Dublin, 1878), iii, p. 254; J.B. Leslie, *Clergy of Connor: from patrician times to the present day* (Belfast, 1993), p. 643.

2   Quotation from John Brady (ed.), 'Remedies proposed for the Church of Ireland (1697)', *Archivium Hibernicum*, 22 (1959), 163–73, at p. 164; 4 William and Mary c. 2; William King, *The state of the Protestants of Ireland under the late King James's government in which their carriage towards him is justified, and the absolute necessity of their endeavouring to be freed from his government, and of submitting to their present Majesties is demonstrated* (London, 1691), pp 233, 235; J.G. Simms, 'The establishment of Protestant Ascendancy, 1691–1714' in T.W. Moody and W.E. Vaughan (eds), *A new history of Ireland*: iv, *Eighteenth-century Ireland* (Oxford, 2009), pp 21–6.

3   T.C. Barnard, 'The uses of 23 October 1641 and Irish Protestant celebrations' *English Historical Review*, 106 (1991), 889–920; T.C. Barnard, 'Reforming Irish manners: the religious societies in Dublin during the 1690s', *Historical Journal*, 35:4 (1992), 805–38; John Gibney, *The shadow of a year: 1641 rebellion in Irish history and memory* (London, 2013), pp 42–3; Edward Wetenhall, *A sermon preached Octob 23 1692* (1692); quotation from Edward Walkington, *A sermon preached Octob. 23 1692 in St Andrew Church* (Dublin, 1692), p. 18.

4   David Dickson, *New foundations: Ireland 1660–1800* (Dublin, 1987), pp 53–5; Tim Harris, *Revolution: the great crisis of the British monarchy, 1685–1720* (London, 2006), pp 506–7; Richard Mant, *History of the Church of Ireland, from the revolution to the union of the churches of England and Ireland, January 1, 1801* (2 vols, London, 1840), ii, pp 42–3; quotation from Walter Alison Phillips, *History of the Church of Ireland from the earliest times to the present day* (3 vols, Oxford, 1933), i, p. 168.

5   RCBL, MS 566.

I. THE LOCAL AND RELIGIOUS WORLD OF THOMAS WARD

1   Laurence Echard, *An exact description of Ireland* (London, 1691), p. 55; R.T. Ridley, 'Echard, Laurence' in *ODNB*, accessed 26 Sept. 2015.

2   Terrier for Glenarm barony from downsurvey.tcd.ie consulted online 24 Aug. 2015; an account in the 1680s claimed that it was only four hours sailing between Carrickfergus and Portpatrick. George Hill, *An historical account of the MacDonnells of Antrim* (Belfast, 1873), p. 379.

3   Terrier for Kilconway barony from www.downsurvey.tcd.ie accessed 24 Aug. 2015.

4   Terrier for Kinalearty barony from www.downsurvey.tcd.ie accessed 24 Aug. 2015.

5   Terrier for Glenarm barony and Lower
    Iveagh barony from www.downsurvey.
    tcd.ie accessed 24 Aug. 2015.
6   Raymond Gillespie, 'Continuity and
    change: Ulster in the seventeenth
    century' in Ciaran Brady, Mary O'Dowd
    and Brian Walker (eds), *Ulster: an
    illustrated history* (London, 1989), p. 119;
    Donald Mac Raild and Malcolm Smith,
    'Migration and emigration, 1600–1945' in
    Liam Kennedy and Philip Ollerenshaw
    (eds), *Ulster since 1600: politics, economy and
    society* (Oxford, 2013), p. 143.
7   Raymond Gillespie, 'The social world of
    County Down in the seventeenth century'
    in Lindsay Proudfoot (ed.), *Down: history
    and society* (Dublin, 1997), p. 143.
8   Patrick Kelly, 'Molyneux, William' in
    DIB, accessed 9 Apr. 2014.
9   Hill, *An historical account*, p. 378.
10 Ibid., pp 378–9.
11 Ibid., p. 382.
12 Gillespie, 'Continuity and change', pp
    125–6.
13 Sean Connolly, *Religion, law and power:
    the making of Protestant Ireland* (Oxford,
    1995), pp 180–1.
14 RCBL, GS 2/7/3/27, f. 43.
15 RCBL, GS 2/7/3/27, f. 39; see also Kilclief
    parish, f. 40, Crumlin parish, f. 42.
16 'State of the dioceses of Down and
    Connor, 1693' (RCBL, GS2/7/3/27,
    f. 176).
17 RCBL, GS 2/7/3/27, f. 50.
18 Ibid., ff 51, 57 (Grange and Bangor).
19 Ibid., f. 49.
20 Ibid., f. 56 (Newton parish); ff 57–8
    (Hollywood).
21 Ibid., ff 15, 40, 42, 45.
22 Ibid., f. 90; see also: RCBL, GS 2/7/3/20,
    p. 26; RCBL, GS 2/7/3/20, p. 62.
23 RCBL, GS 2/7/3/27, ff 92, 94–5, 96, 97,
    99–100.
24 Ibid., ff 64, 147.
25 Ibid., f. 150.
26 James McGuire, 'Taylor, Jeremy' in *DIB*,
    accessed 24 Aug. 2015.
27 Ibid.; Richard Greaves, '"That's no good
    religion that disturbs government": the
    Church of Ireland and the nonconformist
    challenge' in Alan Ford, James McGuire
    and Kenneth Milne (eds), *As by law
    established: the Church of Ireland since the
    Reformation* (Dublin, 1995), pp 121–2.
28 Raymond Gillespie, 'Popular and
    unpopular religion: a view from early
    modern Ireland' in James Donnelly and
    Kerby Miller (eds), *Irish popular culture,
    1650–1850* (Dublin, 1998), pp 32, 45;
    Raymond Gillespie, 'The religion of
    Irish Protestants: a view from the laity,
    1580–1700' in Ford, McGuire and Milne
    (eds), *As by law established*, pp 89–92.
29 Joseph Glanvill, *Saducismus triumphatus,
    or, full and plain evidence concerning witches
    and apparitions in two parts: the first treating
    of their possibility, the second of their real
    existence* (London, 1680), pp 276–91; Phil
    Kilroy, 'Conway, Anne' in *DIB*, accessed
    25 Aug. 2015; Raymond Gillespie,
    *Devoted people: belief and religion in early
    modern Ireland* (Manchester, 1997), pp
    9–10, 110.
30 W.D. Killen (ed.), *A true narrative of the
    rise and progress of the Presbyterian Church in
    Ireland 1623–1670 by the Rev Patrick Adair
    Minister of Belfast* (Belfast, 1866),
    pp 258–9.
31 Hill, *An historical account*, pp 383–4.
32 Ibid., pp 380–1.
33 'Transcript of the visitation of Connor
    in 1694' (RCBL, MS 31/5, ff 297–301).
34 'State of the dioceses of Down and
    Connor, 1693' (RCBL, GS 2/7/3/27,
    ff 173–86, quotations from ff 174, 175
    respectively).
35 John Bergin, 'Hackett, Thomas' in *DIB*,
    accessed 26 Aug. 2015.
36 J.G. Simms, 'The establishment of the
    Protestant Ascendancy, 1691–1714' in
    T.W. Moody and W.E. Vaughan (eds), *A
    new history of Ireland; iv, eighteenth-century
    Ireland, 1691–1800* (Oxford, 2009), pp
    21–2.
37 The National Archives Kew, SP 63/335,
    ff 287–290v.
38 The bishop of Dromore was named
    in the commission but did not
    partake.
39 James McGuire, 'Dopping, Anthony' in
    DIB, accessed 26 Aug. 2015.
40 William King to [Sam Foley], 9 May
    1693 (TCD, MS 1995–2008/274).
41 William King to Samuel Foley, 28 Apr.
    1693 (TCD, MS 1995–2008/273).
42 NAI, Wyche Papers, 2–466–12, item 178,
    p. 1.
43 Bergin, 'Hackett, Thomas'.

44 NAI, Wyche Papers, 2–466–12, item 178, p. 2.

45 Ibid., p. 3.

46 Ibid., p. 21.

47 Ibid., p. 23.

48 Ibid., p. 9.

49 Ibid., pp 10–11; *The book of common-prayer, and administration of the sacraments, and other rites & ceremonies of the Church, according to the use of the Church of Ireland; together with the Psalter or Psalms of David, pointed as they are to be sung or said in churches. And the form and manner of making, ordaining, and consecrating of bishops, priests, & deacons* (Dublin, 1680), 'The ordering of priests', Sig. Rr2.

50 NAI, Wyche Papers, 2–466–12, item 178, p. 10.

51 Bergin, 'Hackett, Thomas'.

52 Leslie, *Clergy of Connor*, pp 490–1.

53 *The proceedings against Archdeacon Lemuel Matthews* (London, 1703), pp 1–2.

54 Matthews later claimed that many of these witnesses 'disowned those depositions as contrary to the truth of fact': Lemuel Matthews, *A letter to the Right Reverend William Lord Bishop of Derry* ([London?], 1703), p. 4.

55 *Proceedings against Archdeacon Lemuel Matthews*, pp 5–8, quotation from p. 6.

56 Ibid., p. 6; Lemuel Matthews, *A letter to the Right Reverend William Lord*, p. 3.

57 *Proceedings against Archdeacon Lemuel Matthews*, p. 8.

58 Ibid., p. 9.

59 Ibid., pp 10–11.

60 Ibid., pp 3–4.

61 Ibid., p. 13.

62 Ibid., p. 14.

63 Ibid., pp 17–18.

64 Ibid., p. 19.

65 Ibid., pp 19–20.

66 Ibid., pp 20–1.

67 Ibid., pp 46–8.

68 'A brief or summary of the proceeding of their majesties ecclesiastical commissioner in their late visitation of the dioceses of Down and Connor against severall of the clergy of the said dioceses' (BL, Lansdowne MS 446, ff 125v, 127); quotation from L. Matthews, *A letter to the Right Reverend William Lord*, p. 13.

69 Matthews published extensively on this matter: *The petition of Archdeacon Matthews to the hon. the commons* (n.d.); *A letter to the Right Reverend William lord bishop of Derry written by Archdeacon Lemuel Matthews* (1703); *Demonstrations that the lord chancellor of Ireland is bound by the statute and common-law and also by his commission and oath … to grant a commission of delegates to Archdeacon Matthews … With replies to the objections* (1704); *The argument of Archdeacon Matthews for a commission of delegates upon his appeals and querel of nullities* (1704); *Remarks on the late printed demonstrations, shewing that the lord chancellor of Ireland ought to grant a commission of delegates to Archdeacon Matthews* (1704); *A brief of the printed argument of Archdeacon Matthews on his petition to the lord chancellor of Ireland for a commission of delegates upon his appeals and querel of nullities against Lisburn-commissioners ecclesiastical* (1705).

70 *To the Honourable the Commons of England in parliament assembled: the humble petition of Lemuel Matthews, Doctor of Divinity, Archdeacon and Chancellor of the diocese of Down, and Prebendary of Carncastle in the diocese of Connor in the kingdom of Ireland* ([London?], 1702), Sig B–Bv.

71 'William and Mary, 1688: *An Act declaring the Rights and Liberties of the Subject and Setleing the Succession of the Crowne*; www.british-history.ac.uk/statutes-realm/vol6/pp142–5, accessed 7 Sept. 2015.

72 *The humble petition of Lemuel Matthews*, Sig B–Bv.

73 William Molyneux, *The case of Ireland's being bound by acts of parliament in England, stated* (Dublin, 1698), pp 76–7.

74 *The humble petition of Lemuel Matthews*, p. 3.

75 NAI, Wyche Papers, 2–466–12, item 179; John Bergin, 'Wyche, Sir Cyril' in *DIB*, accessed 4 Sept. 2015.

76 Matthews, *A Letter to the Right Reverend William Lord Bishop of Derry*, title page verso.

77 Ibid., p. 13.

78 Ibid., p. 9.

79 Ibid., p. 26.

80 Anthony Dopping to Lord Massereene, 2 March 1694 (BL, Add MSS 38,856, f. 110).

2. FAME, REPUTATION AND TALK IN EAST
ULSTER

1 NAI, Wyche Papers, 2–466–12, item 178,
   p. 12.
2 Ibid., pp 16–17.
3 Thelma Fenster and Daniel Lord Smail,
   'Introduction' in Thelma Fenster and
   Daniel Smail (eds), *Fama: the politics of talk
   and reputation in medieval Europe* (London,
   2003), pp 1–14; Adam Fox, *Oral and
   literate culture in England, 1500–1700*
   (Oxford, 2000), pp 1–50; Eamon Darcy,
   'The social order of the 1641 rebellion'
   in Eamon Darcy, Annaleigh Margey and
   Elaine Murphy (eds), *The 1641 depositions
   and the Irish rebellion* (London, 2012), pp
   107–8.
4 Richard Bolton, *A justice of peace for
   Ireland* (Dublin, 1638), p. 29.
5 Ibid., p. 115.
6 NAI, Wyche Papers, 2–466–12, item 178,
   pp 3, 11.
7 Cotton, *Fasti ecclesiae Hibernicae*, ii,
   p. 281; Cotton, *Fasti ecclesiae Hibernicae*,
   iii, pp 254, 319; Leslie, *Clergy of Connor*,
   p. 643.
8 RCBL, MS 566, pp 37–9, quotation from
   p. 39.
9 Ibid., pp 40–2.
10 NAI, Wyche Papers, 2–466–12, item 177.
11 RCBL, MS 566, p. 42.
12 Ibid., p. 1.
13 Ibid., pp 51–2.
14 Ibid., pp 76, 77.
15 Ibid., p. 54.
16 Ibid., pp 56–9.
17 Ibid., pp 60–1.
18 Ibid., p. 79.
19 Ibid., p. 80.
20 Ibid., p. 81.
21 Ibid., p. 61.
22 Ibid., pp 63–6.
23 Ibid., p. 81.
24 Ibid., pp 75–6, 77.
25 Ibid., p. 85.
26 Ibid., p. 88.
27 Ibid., p. 91.
28 Ibid., p. 89.
29 Ibid., p. 92.
30 Madeline H. Caviness and Charles G.
   Nelson, 'Witnesses, women, and courts
   in Medieval Germany' in Fenster and
   Smail (eds), *Fama*, p. 56.
31 Thomas Kuehn, 'Fama as a legal status
   in Renaissance Florence' in Fenster and
   Smail (eds), *Fama*, p. 45.
32 Jeffrey Bowman, 'Infamy and proof in
   medieval Spain' in Fenster and Daniel
   Smail (eds), *Fama*, pp 95–6.
33 NAI, Wyche Papers, 2–466–12, item 178,
   pp 22, 23.
34 Ibid., pp 24–5.
35 'State of the dioceses of Down and
   Connor, 1693', RCBL, GS 2/7/3/27, f.
   176.
36 RCBL, GS 2/7/3/27, f. 186.
37 *Proceedings against Archdeacon Lemuel
   Matthews*, p. 83.
38 Ibid., pp 83–6.
39 Ibid., p. 73.
40 Ibid., p. 80.
41 Ibid., pp 79–80, 82.
42 Ibid., pp 77, 80.
43 Ibid., p. 81.
44 RCBL, MS 566, pp 72–4.
45 Ibid., p. 68.
46 Ibid., p. 69.
47 'State of the dioceses of Down and
   Connor, 1693', RCBL, GS 2/7/3/27, f. 180.
48 RCBL, MS 566, p. 71.
49 Ibid., p. 70.
50 Ibid., p. 68.
51 Ibid., p. 72.
52 Ibid., p. 6.
53 Ibid., p. 8.
54 Ibid., p. 83.
55 Ibid., pp 2, 5.
56 Ibid., pp 31–2.
57 Ibid., p. 16.
58 Ibid., pp 17–19.
59 Ibid., p. 43.
60 Ibid., p. 44.
61 Ibid., p. 43.
62 Ibid., p. 33.
63 Ibid., p. 11.
64 Ibid., pp 11–12.
65 Ibid., p. 3.
66 Ibid., p. 5.
67 Ibid., p. 22.
68 Ibid., p. 44.
69 Ibid.

3. SEX AND SOCIETY IN EAST ULSTER

1 Sean Connolly, 'Illegitimacy and pre-
   nuptial pregnancy in Ireland before 1864:
   the evidence from some Catholic parish

registers', *Irish Economic and Social History*, 6 (1979), 5–23; Anne O'Connor, 'Women in Irish folklore: the testimony regarding illegitimacy, abortion and infanticide' in Margaret MacCurtain and Mary O'Dowd (eds), *Women in early modern Ireland* (Edinburgh, 1991), pp 304–17.

2 Leah Leneman and Rosalind Mitchison, 'Girls in trouble: the social and geographical setting of illegitimacy in early modern Scotland', *Journal of Social History* 21:3, (1988), 495.

3 Deposition of Thomas Fleetwood, 22 Mar. 1643 (TCD, MS 817, f. 39v); Deposition of Elizabeth Gough, 8 Feb. 1642 (TCD, MS 833, f. 2); Deposition of Thomas Greene and Elizabeth Greene, 10 Nov. 1643 (TCD, MS 836, f. 94v); Examination of Winyfrid Field, 18 Oct. 1652 (TCD, MS 816, f. 240); Examination of Martin Nangle, 9 Nov. 1652 (TCD, MS 816, f. 246).

4 Edward Synge, *A defence of the establish'd church and laws* (Dublin, 1705), pp 47–8.

5 Examination of Isabell Kerr, 1 Mar. 1653 (TCD, MS 838, f. 51); Examination of Tirlagh McRichard O'Cahan, 25 Mar. 1653 (TCD, MS 838, f. 84v); Deposition of John Buckner, 7 May 1642 (TCD, MS 818, f. 99v); Peter Laslett, 'The bastardy prone sub-society' in Peter Laslett, Karla Osterveen and Richard Smith (eds), *Bastardy and its comparative history* (Cambridge, 1980), pp 217–39.

6 RCBL, MS 566, p. 12.

7 Ibid., pp 33–4.

8 Ibid., pp 18–22.

9 Fergus Kelly, *A guide to early Irish law* (Dublin, 1988), p. 85.

10 Historical Manuscripts Commission, *Tenth report, appendix, Part V*, (London, 1885), p. 398.

11 18 Elizabeth I c.3; John Briggs, Christopher Harrison, Angus McInnes and David Vincent, *Crime and punishment in England: an introductory history* (London, 1996), p. 38; Faramerz Dabhoiwala, *The origins of sex: a history of the first sexual revolution* (Oxford, 2012), p. 13.

12 RCBL, MS 566, p. 12.

13 James Wolveridge, *Speculum matricis Hybernicum; or the Irish midwives handmaid* (London, 1670), p. 27.

14 Thomas Chamberlayne, *The compleat midwifes practice, in the most weighty and high concernments of the birth of man* (London, 1656), pp 75–6; Nicholas Culpeper, *A directory for midwives: or a guide for women* (London, 1652), 'To the midwives of England'.

15 Keith Wrightson, *English society, 1580–1680* (London, 2000), p. 86.

16 Examination of Ann Whiterly, 9 Mar. 1688 (TCD, MUN/P/1/540).

17 Bernard Capp, 'Republican reformation: family, community and the state in Interregnum Middlesex, 1649–60' in Helen Berry and Elizabeth Foyster (eds), *The family in early modern England* (Cambridge, 2007), p. 55.

18 Leah Lineman and Rosalind Mitchison, *Sin in the city: sexuality and social control in urban Scotland* (Edinburgh, 1998), p. 53.

19 RCBL, MS 566, p. 18. Chapman's story was later corroborated (with the exception of the difficult labour) by Agnus Glascow, RCBL, MS 566, pp 19–20.

20 RCBL, MS 566, p. 8; Samuel Thomas, 'Early modern midwifery: splitting the profession, connecting the history', *Journal of Social History*, 43:1 (2009), p. 121, argues that midwives who helped with the birth of illegitimate children were probably less wealthy than those who refused to help.

21 RCBL, MS 566, pp 34–5.

22 Malcolm Gaskill, 'Reporting murder: fiction in the archives in early modern England', *Social History*, 23 (1998), 8–10.

23 RCBL, MS 566, p. 7; see also the testimony of Elizabeth Johnson who alleged that Ann Wilson told her that Ward fathered her child. RCBL, MS 566, p. 10. Similarly, Ann Kidd deposed that Margaret Higgins confessed 'many' times that Ward fathered her child, RCBL, MS 566, f. 18.

24 RCBL, MS 566, pp 8–9.

25 Ibid., pp 12–13 (quotation on p. 12).

26 Ibid., p. 15.

27 Ibid., pp 19–20.

28 Ibid., pp 34–5.

29 Ibid., p. 5, point repeated on p. 22.

30 Ibid., p. 13. The naming of illegitimate children after their father was common practice in Irish society until the 17th

century, see: Kenneth Nicholls, *Gaelic and Gaelicised Ireland in the Middle Ages* (Dublin, 2003), pp 88–90.

31 RCBL, MS 566, pp 20–1.

32 The accusation that women had given birth to (m)any illegitimate was commonly used to discredit them and cast further aspersions on their character. Deposition of Joseph Wheeler et al., 5 July 1643 (TCD, MS 812, f. 203).

33 RCBL, MS 566, p. 66.

34 Examination of Anthony Heard, 29 Jan. 1687 (TCD, MUN/P/1/527).

35 RCBL, MS 566, p. 10, see also pp 12–13.

36 'The introduction to the book of genealogies, by Dubhaltach Mac Firbhisigh' in Toirdhealbhach Ó Raithbheartaigh (ed.), *Genealogical tracts I* (Dublin, 1932), p. 25.

37 BL, Harl MS 5999, f. 32; Kelly, *A guide to early Irish law*, p. 79; See also: Aidan Clarke, 'The 1641 rebellion and anti-popery in Ireland' in Brian MacCuarta (ed.), *Ulster 1641: aspects of the rising* (Belfast, 1993), pp 139–58; Kathleen Noonan, '"The cruell pressure of an enraged, barbarous people": Irish and English identity in seventeenth-century policy and propaganda', *Historical Journal*, 41:1 (1998), 151–77.

38 Richard Bolton, *A Justice of Peace for Ireland, consisting of two Bookes: the first declaring the exercise of that office by one of more Iustices of Peace out of sessions. The second setting forth the form and proceeding in Sessions, and the matters to be enquired of, and handled therein* (Dublin, 1638), pp 100–1; Kelly, *Guide to early Irish law*, p. 85.

39 RCBL, MS 566, pp 16–17.

40 Ibid., pp 22–4.

41 Ibid., p. 28.

42 Ibid., p. 22.

43 Ibid., p. 30.

44 'An abstract of acts brought over by Sir H Winch and Sir J Davys' (*CSPI 1611–14*, p. 249).

45 'Abstract of the sums which the Pope annually extracts from Ireland' (*CSPI 1647–1660*, p. 299); Raymond Gillespie, 'Catholic religious practices and payments in seventeenth-century Ireland', *Archivium Hibernicum* 47 (1993), 3–10.

46 Robert Dunlop (ed.), *Ireland under the Commonwealth* (2 vols, Manchester, 1913), i, no. 997; this reflected events in the wider three kingdoms. Bernard Capp has argued that by 1659 there were clear indications that Puritan discipline was weakening: Capp, 'Republican reformation', p. 66.

47 RCBL, MS 566, p. 3.

48 Ibid., pp 8–9.

49 Charles Leslie, *A letter of advice to a friend upon the modern argument of the lawfullness of simple fornication, half-adultery, and polygamy* (London, 1696), quotation from p. 6.

50 Dudley Loftus, *The case of Ware and Sherley as it was set forth in matter of fact* (Dublin, 1669), p. 10.

51 Jane Ohlmeyer, *Making Ireland English: the Irish aristocracy in the seventeenth century* (New Haven, 2012), pp 171–3.

52 Francis Boyle, *Discourses useful for the vain modish ladies and their gallants* (London, 1696), pp 2, 3, 4, 59.

53 John Jones to Col. Robert Phayre, 29 July 1653 (Historical Manuscripts Commission, *Egmont*, vol. i, p. 523).

54 William King to unknown, 8 June 1694 (TCD, MS 1995–2008/358a).

55 RCBL, MS 566, f. 28.

56 Ibid., f. 25.

57 Ibid., ff 26–7.

CONCLUSION

1 'A brief or summary of the proceeding of their majesties ecclesiastical commissioner in their late visitation of the dioceses of Down and Connor against severall of the clergy of the said dioceses' (BL, Lansdowne MS 446, ff 125–7v).

2 'State of the dioceses of Down and Connor, 1693' (RCBL, GS 2/7/3/27, ff 173–86, f. 174).

3 Margaret MacCurtain and Mary O'Dowd (eds), *Women in early modern Ireland* (Dublin, 1991); Mary O'Dowd, *A history of women in Ireland, 1500–1800* (London, 2004); Rachel Wilson, *Elite women in Ascendancy Ireland, 1690–1745* (Woodbridge, 2015).